Russell James Ray is an Early Childhood Educator living in Santa Fe, New Mexico, where he is a single father and striving artist interested in all manners of coupling intellectual thoughts with physical pursuits. Mountain climbing and canoeing are his favorite physical diversions from Scientific musings. For him the world is a mysterious place of wonder where he likes to immerse his spiritual and corporeal self.

Russell James Ray

CANYONS OF THE MIND

AUSTIN MACAULEY PUBLISHERS™
LONDON • CAMBRIDGE • NEW YORK • SHARJAH

Ordering Information
Quantity sales: Special discounts are available on quantity purchases by corporations, associations, and others. For details, contact the publisher at the address below.

Publisher's Cataloging-in-Publication data
James Ray, Russell
Canyons of the Mind

ISBN 9781638292111 (Paperback)
ISBN 9781638292128 (Hardback)
ISBN 9781638292142 (ePub e-book)
ISBN 9781638292135 (Audiobook)

Library of Congress Control Number: 2022921278

www.austinmacauley.com/us

First Published 2023
Austin Macauley Publishers LLC
40 Wall Street, 33rd Floor, Suite 3302
New York, NY 10005
USA

mail-usa@austinmacauley.com
+1 (646) 5125767

Dedicated to the memory of Patrick Braxton-Andrew.

My immense respect and gratitude go out to my amazing canyoneering partners: Dean Bruemmer and Scott Steinberg. I gratefully acknowledge the kind and patient mentoring that Susan Engbring brought to editing my manuscript as well as her design of the book cover. 1987 saw the first of my sojourns into the wilds of Copper Canyon. It also saw the last of the great Dick Griffith's adventures in Barranca del Cobre. His ill-fated trip juxtaposed the start of my marvelous long adventure. Dick jokingly inquired as to why our paths had not crossed in the vast canyon area. Temporal proximity had surrendered to spatial constraints. My immense gratitude of Dick leading the way transcends time and space.

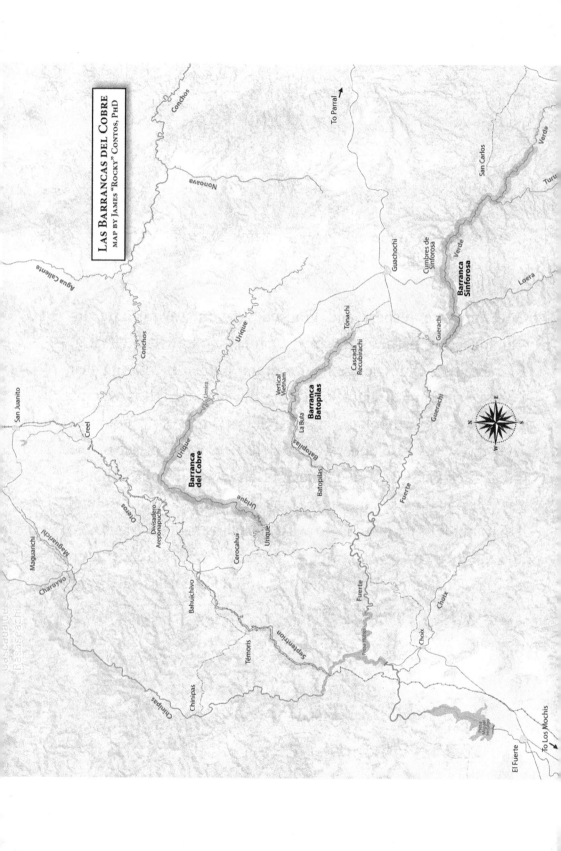

LAS BARRANCAS DEL COBRE
MAP BY JAMES "ROCKY" CONTOS, PhD

Table of Contents

Foreword

What "rustyjames" has done is an entirely different method of going down an unexplored canyon. Most Canyoneers have used a boat or, at the very minimal, a pack raft. The photos show that it would be easy to become trapped, not able to go forward or backward. You would have to be a skilled rock climber. With rope going down, it is possible to rappel, but how do you go back? Rusty has done the Barranca de Cobre the same as I, but that canyon does not have the serious water crossings as the rest of the canyons. I know of no one that has ever made an attempt at all of these canyons. Most people do not have the required skills even if they wanted to.

Dick Griffith

Introduction

1987 had me starting down a long path of connecting the dots of a geographic location with time-space addresses. It was the start of a major phase in my life that had commenced with a meeting of the Western New Mexico University Outdoor Club. A suggestion of going to Copper Canyon for a spring break Club adventure trip was proposed by my friend Jody. I said, "Great, where's that?" To say the rest is history suggests a denial that I still fantasize of a return trip to the Upper Barranca del Cobre in order to dovetail with the 1.5 times I have descended that canyon already.

In the ensuing years, successful descents of the Barranca del Cobre (Copper Canyon), the Barranca Sinforosa, and the Barranca Batopilas would have me go on to be a written-about canyon explorer. The descents of the Sinforosa and Batopilas are considered the first time those great canyons had been traversed utilizing canyoneering techniques. The '87 spring break trip yielded a simple descent into Copper Canyon (Barranca del Cobre) at a point a couple of miles past Divisadero. At the village of Areponapuchi, there exists a trail that I have since gone on to tread a total of seven times. The cosmic happenstance of discovering this trail I have long since given up trying to explain. A part of me just seemed to know where to go. Besides the recurrent strong fantasy of completing two full descents of the Barranca Del Cobre from the bridge at Umira all the way to the village of Urique, my life will forever be affected in a major and unshakable way by the reverberations of that canyon. It is now a permanent fixture of my body and soul. I have two sons born of my time spent in the Barranca del Cobre. Their mother from Spain came into my life in a cosmic meeting down in the Copper Canyon country. I will love her for all time. I feel the canyons in my knees, and my mind flashes on the memories of the elation and hardships experienced during the canyon years.

The canyon years can be distilled to 1991-1994, but that would be leaving out the vapors of 1987, 1990, 2001, 2002, 2003, and 2004. All these years contain dates that constitute time spent in the geographic location known as "The Copper Canyon." To me, a delineation has become thinking in terms of "Las Barrancas del Cobre": Barranca del Cobre, Barranca Sinforosa, and Barranca Batopilas. While it is true that there are other barrancas, with the Barranca Otero and Barranca Guaynopa having occupied some of my exploratory efforts, it is mainly the three sister rivers of the Rio Fuerte that really took hold of those efforts. 1987 didn't really serve to wet my appetite, but 1990 certainly did. 1987 was simply a descent to the Rio Urique with a group of friends that included two women and three children as well as myself and a male friend of mine who was out of Kansas City. 1990 had me armed with Richard D. Fisher's book, *National Parks of Northwest Mexico* (1988), written to include Copper Canyon. While I didn't treat the book as Gospel, it definitely influenced me to descend at Areponapuchi and traverse up the River Urique approximately seven miles to a canyon exit at the eye of the canyon trail up to Divisadero.

It was during this trip which included four women and three men, that I began to think of this canyon as more than a passing fancy. I began to envision what a new pursuit I had become aware of, called "canyoneering," must surely entail. Number one should certainly be descending the river, not ascending it, as scientifically speaking, the gravity involved in a non-M.C. Escher river flow should aid the ability to travel the river bottom. By 1991 I had it in mind to descend the Rio Urique from the bridge at Umira all the way to the village of Urique. In the book I had stated this had never been done before and that it was impassible. I realized that while it is true that I could not fly to the moon, it seemed obvious that others could do it. What was to stop me from trying? Fear of the unknown didn't factor into my scheme despite my ex-wife's pleading that I just believe Rick Fisher's accounting on this geographic location.

As circumstances would unfold, I fortuitously joined with two stalwart partners who would go on to accompany me on descents of the Barrancas del Cobre, Sinforosa, and Batopilas. This effort took a total of four expeditions to accomplish descending the three sister barrancas. Attempts at perfecting our style of river travel, "Puro en el Rio," had us adopting waterproof floating backpacks and wetsuits. On average, the packs ended up weighing 80+ pounds, as the expeditions took an average of two weeks of unresupplied effort to make it through each of the barrancas, starting top to stopping bottom. Making it through entailed traversing what we deemed to be the "technical" stretches of the canyons, as with each canyon, the sections above and below our efforts appear to constitute terrain that can potentially be traveled down via rafting or hiking without an appreciable amount of "canyoneering" involved. As my hat is off to the folks truly pushing the boundaries of canyoneering in slot canyons throughout the world, I will confess to scant experience along those lines. While it is true that I have been in several slot canyons, and I did pass through Buckskin Gulch, which at 15 miles long is said to be the longest slot canyon in the world.

My interest was, in reality, limited to the large barrancas. With them, I have long since tired of comparisons with the Grand Canyon. The Grand Canyon is incredibly gorgeous and immense, as well as having the righteous Colorado River flowing through it. The Colorado River drops an average of 25 ft. per mile, thus lending itself to rafting. The barrancas drop an average of 125 ft. per mile and are not as voluminous as the Colorado River. They really don't lend themselves to rafting unless it is pack rafting. Though they are capable of raging in flood, I would not want to be around for that roller coaster ride. In the timeframe that we descended the barrancas, it seems that kayaking equipment and techniques had yet to come into their current and awesome potential. Just Google the exploits of James "Rocky" Contos to be schooled in the realm of current kayaking possibilities and learn what he has accomplished in the barrancas and elsewhere. With the Grand Canyon, I did a day hike to Phantom Ranch and back up, as well as fought fires on both the North and South Rims, but I was never really attracted to that canyon-like my strange attractor, Las Barrancas del Cobre. Who can really elaborate on a personal decision to accomplish an exploratory endeavor beyond the clichéd axiom, "Because it was there"? Perhaps that is it, coupled with the desire to see the unknown and unseen segments of our incredibly beautiful Planet Earth.

In the case of my dealings with this massive canyon system, I must confess to not only doubting my own soundness of mind but having others do that also. I don't choose to use the term obsessed, as I like to think I was capably determined. Events swirling about my life had me not always making the soundest of decisions. Others involved in these endeavors may have differing historical recounting of events and motivations. The decisions to descend these canyons, when looked at objectively, constitute a large part of a life lived largely. As I am the one writing this book, this is my tale.

Prologue
The Beginning and End

The karmic significance of being conceived in Chama, New Mexico, and then being born in the State of Mississippi has always had me curious regarding astrological as well as demographical parts of a puzzle. As a scientist, the demographics are easy enough to peg via statistical analysis, as New Mexico and Mississippi vie neck and neck to be number one at the bottom of many yardsticks of measure. However, with astrological ramifications, the Airy-Fairy nature of that subset perspective has proven an elusive grasping of cosmological considerations impossible to fully elucidate. As a scientist, the pragmatics of empirical thinking generally leads to attempts at objectifying the subjective.

As I sit writing this chapter in the ever so peaceful Gila River valley at the Wilderness Lodge, a place owned by my dear friends Dean and Jane Bruemmer, memories of the canyon years can be augmented by the recollections of others in this geographic location which never fails to provide solace. Both Dean and Jane played integral roles in my canyoneering exploits. Also, here I can be freed up to more fully remember my life of the outdoors. Memories come as I feel the breeze while looking at the verdant world. A life that had begun in Mississippi, a geographic location which apparently provided what my soul came into this earthly plain of existence desiring.

All I really wanted was to be outdoors, where exhibiting Tom Sawyer's behaviors came as natural as breathing to me. Hours were spent exploring the woods and the waterways, hunting snakes, turtles, and mud ducks. Fishing on the Gulf of Mexico and securing a storm-washed boat fostered a pseudo-pirate's existence. Outdoors is where I felt a sense of belonging, as being half Mexican while Mississippi burned had me treated as an outsider. I never affected the Southern drawl. I was told, "We're Americans what are you?" My schooling in Mississippi had them diagnosing me as being retarded, and that my parents should never expect much from me in the academic department. I remember a sense of relief, as it meant they would leave me to daydream and adventure. I played that diagnosis through many years of adventuring before eventually teaching myself to read, and that allowed me to graduate after 12 years of school drudgery. I went on to attend college, where I majored in science.

As a child, my father was in the military, and that lifestyle fed my wanderlust to see the world. Two years spent in the Philippines meant jungle exploration and the beginnings of a tendency toward pyromania. Living amongst the redwoods, situated on the high cliffs above the Pacific Ocean at the mouth of the Klamath River, had me gain an intimate understanding of just what it meant to potentially die of exposure. The concept of "death by exposure" fascinated me. The Sonoran Desert of Arizona further brought home the lessons to be learned naturalistically in the School of the Great Outdoors. Upon leaving college without graduating, as I had taken only science classes, I felt prepared to dive headlong into the application of my science education. I had treated college as a Renaissance vocational opportunity. Fortuitously, I had served a stint fighting wildland fires immediately after leaving college, and seemingly a die was cast. I would commonly daydream of life of the outdoors while functioning as a microbiologist in Kansas City, Missouri, where my ex-wife and I had located to live so she could attend dental school. Upon her graduating in 1984, we migrated back to New Mexico, where I became a member of a U.S. Fish and Wildlife Fire Engine Crew on the Bosque del Apache Wildlife Refuge.

We then moved to Silver City, New Mexico, where she could practice dentistry. I had strongly advocated for Silver City because it was a junky little town where nothing was happening except its close proximity to the Gila National Forest. It was a place that I was compelled towards. A place where I could get out of doors. The need for work necessitated my barging in on a meeting of Gila N.F. Big Wigs to announced my arrival. I told the packed room I would work for them. Alas, it was actually my wife, the dentist, who ended up with a Gila N.F. Dispatcher as a patient that led to me receiving a call to serve as a Seasonal Dispatcher. The seasonal position allowed me to not only learn the topographical scope of the Gila but also to get to know the varied personalities of Gila's employee pool. It led to me becoming an accepted outsider. After that, the door on the Gila was fully opened for me to enter into that world of this great outdoors. I now had options for a wide array of outdoor work pursuits.

A District Ranger I had done a solid for while I was a Dispatcher picked me up to be his Trail Crew Foreman the

an Acoma Indian as we melted in the heat. Being sent to Horse Packing School, dealing with a drunkard deaf wrangler whose hearing aids had melted by the campfire, thus rendering him incapable of perceiving blacktail rattlesnakes. Not that it hadn't been a beautiful season. It was time to wrap it up, all packaged for File 13.

The call came into my lunch-addled brain. Would I go rescue a hunter down in Rain Creek? Sure, it's what I liked, trained as I was. I was a Wilderness EMT and a member of Grant County Search and Rescue. It was all too cool. Better than watching TV, and it was outside. My supervisor said I could respond, and out the door, I went. An initial problem was that Rain Creek was over 30 miles away, and according to the usual scant information I was given on the situation, this man would not be served by some late-ass EMT. He'd been shot, and I couldn't secure a faster helicopter ride out.

Being a member of Search and Rescue wouldn't necessarily get you out of a speeding ticket, and reckless driving is generally frowned upon. Onward I went, hoping providence was on my side. Intent on rendering aid to some stricken soul, I drove a crepuscular sonic flight path. Coming upon roadwork, I flashed my handheld radio serving as a badge in the serious road worker's face. "A rescue to do, man. Someone shot. Precious time ticking away. For Christ's sake!" I had providence on my side as he let me through with only minor consternation.

Up on Rain Creek Mesa, Rescue Base was easily found. They were the ones with a helicopter. After screeching to a stop, I was greeted with, "Ah Russ, you ran my flight helmet over." Not wanting to miss a chance to avoid paying for the damn thing, my adrenaline-charged response poured out, "Screw your helmet. What was it doing camouflaged in the weeds anyhow? Don't we have a man down?"

He was already dead. Turns out he was shot dead. 50-caliber dead. It was time for primitive weapon hunting on the Gila, and this black powder powerhouse had proven quite effective at blowing this man away. It was time to do what is required of these situations, time to drink some coffee and shoot the shit around rescue base while they mustered some others for a body retrieval out of the canyon bottom. I wasn't much down for that activity. I was a Medic.

The coffee-aided briefing revealed the facts: Some hours ago, a 52-year-old man had been out of this fine day with his wife for a bit of sport. She reported an accidental discharge of her weapon, a 50-caliber muzzleloader while crossing a logjam, occurring at close range. Deadly for sure. A problem was that she couldn't remember which trail they had been down when she reported the accident to the first person she chanced upon back on the Mesa. Odd, as only one trail exits on Rain Creek Mesa, the one directly down to Rain Creek, all of a mile's distance away. Someone went to alert the authorities, and someone else headed in the logical direction down to find the 50-caliber victim, who was quite dead lying in Rain Creek. Search and Rescue were now body retrieval-bound, which was always a favorite, as sometimes putrefaction is very hard to stomach.

I had grown bored rather quickly, like an ADD child forced to sit too long, and this event had long since lost any appeal. I was also growing frustrated listening to boys and their toys dictate a helicopter hoisting of the victim out of the canyon bottom. I told them that there was too much risk involved, especially since the body was only a mile away down an easy trail. Men behave like little boys whenever a new toy is introduced into the playground, and a helicopter is a huge, dangerous, and irresistible toy. It is always so tempting to see what one of those babies can do. It didn't take long for me to offer up leading a Stokes Litter team down to carry the body out. Boys and their toys and us versed in the particulars of a hoist, the plan was set. I would take a team down to fly him out.

A medical examiner arrived. This was going to be a new experience for me, as I had never encountered such an authority. She set me at ease by immediately admitting her urban preferences. She didn't know the drill and asked for some help with her investigation. This intrigued me. Three of Search and Rescue's finest set out with the medical examiner in tow. We didn't walk long before the canyon bottom was reached. There he lay, right in the water with a log jam to his side. He looked so peaceful. Even the large hole in his chest couldn't distract me from marveling at the shame of it all. Obviously fit, he had taken care to be robust and handsome on this, the day of his death.

Distraction came soon enough in the form of a Jarhead-looking camo man who made his presence known by stepping out of the foliage and hovering around as I was maneuvered into taking photos and measurements for our urban M.E. I wondered if any of this was legal. Shouldn't her professionally trained shoes be the ones getting wet? The M.E. called a halt to my activity after reaching some known-to-only-her, job-well-done completion point. The Jarhead camo man spoke. It took me by surprise, as I was now lost in private thoughts of this unfortunate man's fate. Who was this beautiful man now lying dead at our feet, the cold water pouring gracefully over his powerful frame, his eyes slightly open, staring up at the blue, blue sky? He appeared to be a cloud set down on the ground, his skin had grown pale as death so obviously inhabited his mortal self.

What was the camo man talking about, telling us how the hoist should go? Who did he think he was, and who the hell was he? I wanted to get the show on the road, so I asked him if he knew this drill. He failed to respond, so I asked him who he was. This got his attention, and he responded, "I'm a State Trooper." That's that: he was the de facto boss. State Troopers are always in charge of any situation in front of them, even ones that escape their abilities. The Jarhead countenance seemed to melt away, as he admitted he didn't know the particulars of a helicopter hoisting. Apparently, he had been running on de facto autopilot as his previous edicts gave way to helping us get the show on the road.

As the M.E. tentatively headed back up the trail, we packaged the body. He was gently placed in a body bag and strapped in the Stokes Litter. I radioed Rescue Base that we were ready for the hoist. The first of my boys and their toys' reservations were realized when the Stokes Litter proceeded more horizontal than vertical. As it snagged a juniper tree, the very real possibility of a downed ship flashed through my mind. If it was a punch-free line our Stokes was hooked to, the helicopter could pull itself down. The Stokes Litter crashed through the juniper branches as the helicopter gunned its engine and got a vertical lift. Slowly the Stokes spun out of sight, and we headed up the trail.

I remember the usual stop at the bar on the way home. I didn't like one of our finest braggings too much, as what had we accomplished, almost bringing down a ship and probably fucking up an investigation?

What I now remember most is an event from the following season. I had gotten away from the danger of any office work. I was now a Wilderness Ranger, with one of my duties being to complete an inventory of all the district's wilderness signs. I had one more sign to inventory, and I would be done. The long beautiful season was coming to an end. A short trip to Rain Creek Mesa, a few photos, and I would be Mexico-bound. The Rain Creek Trail sign was driven right up to, and the job was done. Remembering the body retrieval from the previous season, I decided to hike down to the canyon bottom to pay some kind of last respects. At the canyon bottom, I came upon a man dressed in camo. Strange. I stepped out of the foliage. He turned and spoke. He was there to see the place where his brother had lost his life the previous year, murdered it seemed. Shot with a 50-caliber slug. I offered some words of condolence and headed back up the trail.

The Green Bomber

Considering that I had laid off early the previous season in a funk over not wanting to monitor the activities of potentially errant deer hunters, it was a wonder that I was welcomed back for the 1994 season. I guess they liked the work I did. I was good at my job. Being a Wilderness Ranger can be one travail after another, with moments up high and others down low. If they wanted me to converse with killers, why not arm me to the teeth? As I wore a Forest Service uniform as my only protection from the confusing morass of opinion-driven enjoyment of the outdoors, I had decided the previous season to pass into unemployment bliss. While on patrol, I was expected to be a Joe for all occasions. Some kind of knight in light green armor. I could prove so good at this professional backpacker gig. I was also capable of being very human. I liked being a solitary human. The wilderness is supposed to be about nature, not man. My psychological profile has shown me to be more biocentric than anthropocentric. Still, they liked my work.

For this season, a newfound partner and I constituted an effort by the Forest Service to provide visitor contact. "Visitor" is a term that denotes a person out in the woods. Away from home, they might find themselves in need of Search and Rescue or an intrusive talking to by some Green Knights. The feeling of an out-of-context element may go a long way toward explaining why I had maneuvered last season's activities in a direction that almost excluded visitor contact altogether. Hell, I went days in

'93 without seeing another soul. I was solo then, and I liked it that way. I patrolled the crap out of every remote corner of the Glenwood District. I climbed every high peak I could lay boots on. I cleaned springs. Moved deadfall. I felt as if Heaven really was here on Earth, as the Bible had attempted to tell me so.

This season was going to be different. I had a crew. A crew of two. To crew what? I would have to wait to find that out. It certainly would involve moving heavy deadfall, trail clearing, and other trail crew activities that the General Accounting Office would surely frown upon. Wilderness funds were to be spent on visitor contact, interpretation, education, trail scouting, Search and Rescue, and light trail work. No need for a crew to accomplish that.

Our first shift out had my partner and me going into the wilderness along the familiar Crest Trail, the trail that moves along the spine of the Mogollon Mountains. They are the heart of the Gila Wilderness, a place I had grown to know and love. We would be expected to be out for eight days. We hiked into Hummingbird Saddle, where we set up camp in order to stage day hikes throughout the district. This way, we could cover as much as 24 miles or more a day. We would, this season, try for as much visitor contact as possible.

Camping at Hummingbird Saddle always assured plenty of visitors to contact. They congregate there like a siege. A siege on the wilderness that at times brings to mind the ladybugs that swarm 10,000-foot peaks. Numerous and brightly colored. I was planning to go off shift and just read a book in the privacy of my tent after cooking dinner. Off shift, my time was my own. Off came the light green armor. I settled in for a read in the solitude of nature's library, but the distraction of my partner doing rifle drills with a cut pole damn near made that impossible. He was an ex-Marine and apparently still in the Corps. In his mind, at least. Just a big boy at heart. I zipped my tent shut and gave him no more thought. I always sleep so well in the woods.

The morning sun woke me on high. Hummingbird Saddle sits over 10,000 feet in the air. There the sun never consents to a canyon bottom sleep-in. I never concerned myself with an alarm clock's warning, as the day is inevitably begun. Unzipping my tent, I was greeted by a dream. A dream my partner had during the dark mountain night. He dreamed of killing me in my sleep. This came from him unsolicited and without the benefit of coffee. He went on to explain that no one in his unit could out-hike him. How could I manage such a feat, seeing how I was older than him and a smoker to boot? The day before had seen him lagging, and he could not fathom being bested by me. I put it off to him as differing mountain sense. I suggested we head out for 18 miles to see how it goes.

Our plan was to hike into Mogollon Baldy for a look-see along the Crest Trail. The snow still remained on the northern slopes, but we covered the distance to Mogollon Baldy in fairly good time. I made sure to measure my pace so as not to have my partner dreaming any dreams. The day was so glorious, made more so by boundless freedom found only in the Wilderness. Mogollon Baldy, still packed in snow, is always a welcomed sight. She is a beauty rising above all she surveys. A sentinel, situated at the end of the Crest Trail. The desire to linger was overcome only by the nine-mile hike that separated us from our camp. We both seemed to have the same thoughts. Thoughts of dinner and bed. Thoughts of a first day well done. We headed back to camp along the Crest Trail, and like rental horses, making headed-back-to-camp time.

The Marine was at the point, as this suited the dream plan that I instituted for the duration of this shift. Besides, he had a desire to be at the point. BOOM, an explosion went off, shattering my meditative silence. Smelling gunpowder, I did a quick self-check to ascertain if I was injured before asking my partner if he was all right. He required my asking him again in a louder voice. He responded with, "What was that?" I said, "Don't you smell that?" "War games," he said as his nostrils flared in the gunsmoke. All I needed and wanted to know was if he was injured. I had him stand still for a thorough going over. He was likewise uninjured. We inspected the device he had tripped. It was a monofilament set to trip a small explosion. Someone had rigged it to do just that after we had passed through on our way to Mogollon Baldy. This mighty peculiar practical joke didn't sit well with me. My partner thought it was all just innocent fun. He seemed oblivious to the possible ramifications of such an act. Aside from potential injury, there was the possibility of starting a wildfire, not to mention wilderness etiquette considerations.

At the shift's end, I reported the incident to the district's law enforcement officer. He seemed amused by the story and proceeded to do nothing about it. I was going off shift for six days of a different life, and my thoughts on the matter went out the door as surely as I did. Before leaving, I visited with my supervisor about moving the Marine to the trail crew, where I thought he would be better suited. The dream and the drill were not called upon to convince my boss that he should act administratively on the matter, as apparently, he had already hired two women for me to take out as a crew comes next shift. The Marine would go to work with the trail crew, and I would now have a crew of three.

Working with women is infinitely more interesting than working with men. It would prove more interesting than working alone. Something about short shorts, sweat, and nature. They just seemed to go together. The combination hints of possibilities unknown. We had a lot of work and miles ahead of us, and getting along through thick and thin had always been easier for me when women are involved. My effeminate side is freed from macho constraints. Although it usually works out that women deem me too much a man, still, I fantasize that we share the same mother. Her name is Earth. Men can have a problem with such sentimentality.

The crew got along well durning our first shift out. We pushed many miles of trails with an absolute resolve of getting things done. Trails were cleared of deadfall. Water bars repaired. We closed unused trails. We inventoried and pulled signs. Springs were cleaned, and we met visitors head-on. They always seemed pleased to see female knights. Returning to the District Office after eight days out, we all felt a comradeship that we all hoped would come with our wonderful turf. The season was shaping up to be all it should be.

Before I could get out the door, the District L.E.O. wanted a confab. He asked me about people we had seen at Hummingbird Saddle. "What people?" I asked. "There was nobody there." This was a memory of note, as there are always people there. Their absence had allowed us to finally clean the place up. All the trash was packed out, and the huge fire pits were remade to the appropriate size and number. He then changed his strategy to asking about an off-duty BLM Ranger that we had spoken with. This jogged my memory, as I recalled this individual's desire to chit chat only with the female knights. He and I shared no words, and I quickly put him out of my mind. Turns out he had come in to report a device that was rigged to fire 12-gauge shotgun shells. The dispersal pattern was definitely of a whole different caliber than the previous shift's noisemaker. The BLM Ranger had left the device in place after disarming the monofilament trigger. He came directly into the District Office to report his find.

The field investigation that followed should have signified the beginning of the end for our disturbed prankster. It did not. I had no way of knowing it, but the season would have more and deadlier devices placed out in the Wilderness and visitors left out of the loop. And that the placing of explosive devices would continue into the next season. Instead of interpreting the danger for the visiting public, the Forest Service chose to simply not let on that there was a problem in paradise.

My crew and I had no way of knowing about the deadly device. We had headed out of the Wilderness to the south as we worked our way through our eight-day shift. Nobody had given us a radio heads-up about the device set up somewhere near where the Marine had set off the first explosion. I was angry about the lack of communication. I was even more angered to learn that no investigation had accompanied the first incident. I told the L.E.O. that I had a habit of always noting vehicle license plate numbers at the Crest Trail parking area despite being told that I shouldn't do that. I did it for my own reasons. I thought it was a prudent practice. I offered him the numbers, which he hesitantly took.

In the urban world, I told everyone I knew about the Green Bomber. The season went on with the usual highs and lows. The highs included a lack of fear about being at any more risk than is normally associated with this job. Lightning was a more prevalent concern, and the Green Bomber just didn't fit into the green equation. The lows included being called on the carpet over my biocentric wilderness stance. The local yokel contingent was lodging complaints about what I had been writing in the Apache Cabin log. Apache Cabin is a historic eyesore situated exactly where it shouldn't be, in the Wilderness. I advocated burning the damn thing down (citing hantavirus concerns), as well as other unsavory misanthropic activities. The War on the West was heating up, and lines were being drawn. My supervisor pleaded with me to behave myself. In lieu of doing that, I had my nose pierced. I did consent to wear shoes while in the District Office, but I drew the line at producing a short video promoting anti-nudity while in the hot springs. Nudity and nature seem to get along just fine. Also, the "offense" is not listed in the Code of Federal Regulations.

I concluded the season with the usual emotional fanfare by marrying one of my crew members. We had fallen madly in love. I spoke at length with Gila's big Wilderness boss about my War on the West concerns. She was very receptive and soon to be transferred to some other locale. I went into unemployment bliss. The Green Bomber faded into my green dreams. I gave it all very little more thought.

I was sitting in a bar enjoying unemployment bliss when my direct supervisor for the upcoming 1995 season informed me that Wilderness funding had been cut. I was to come back to serve as Trail Crew Foreman. "No thanks," I said. Been there, done that. I opted to spend the season contracted as a Fireline EMT. I would respond to fire calls, or not, at my discretion. The money was really good, and the War on the West could be waged by those who chose to take a side. I had friends on both sides of the land use issues. Getting caught in the middle always seemed to force me further in the direction of not wanting to choose sides. In my universe, truths are seen as self-evident. I would always speak my truth, convinced that I had no need to defend any particular stance. You either are or are not biocentric. You either are or are not in need of contention in your life. My wife was expecting our baby girl, and all I wanted was to make some money and survive the upcoming fire season.

The fire season went well. I was enjoying the paychecks and the freedom of self-determining my time scheduling. The Wilderness now manifested a smoking face, but I could always see clearly to my life away from the haze.

My brother John and three friends were out on a backpacking tour of the Gila's upper West Fork. They knew that the cylindrical object lying at their feet was obviously out of place. It looked like a bomb. The hip chain was strewn about the creek bed like some web of unknown deceit. The object appeared innocuous enough to them, and they decided to bring it out of the Wilderness, as isn't that what you should do with Wilderness trash? Odd-man-out amongst my brother's hiking group got elected to be the mule. He was forced to walk a distance behind, a bomb in tow, while John and the two women took point on the way out to White Creek Cabin several miles away. After reaching the cabin, the hiking group was more than glad to hand the device over to the Wilderness Ranger in residence. The Ranger, tucking his shirt in, had come to the door of White Creek Cabin to greet these Wilderness visitors head-on. He thanked them for the device and sent them on their way. The Ranger placed the device outside the cabin for three days before hauling it in his backpack for two days out of the Wilderness. Reaching his District Office, he placed it on his supervisor's desk. The supervisor placed the bomb behind the seat of his Forest Service rig and drove into Gila's main law enforcement officer's office. Placing it on the L.E.O.'s desk, he asked, "What's this?" The ensuing bomb scare had Gila's supervisor's office building evacuated.

I learned of this Green Bomber incident after coming off fire when my brother John called to say, "You won't believe what happened." I was amazed, as my thoughts on the Green Bomber were definitely on the back burner, to learn that the Bomber was still active and that Wilderness visitors were still being exposed to superfluous risk. It seemed to me that the matter should have been concluded. At the least, the Forest Service should have warned the public about the explosive devices, warned the visitors not to haul this brand of trash out of the Wilderness.

In front of me is an article from the Albuquerque Journal dated August 2, 1995. The article headline reads, "Agency admits errors handling bombs." "Five explosive devices have been found in the Gila Wilderness. The Forest Service says it mishandled some of those finds." "Five explosive devices,

34

three mistakes, and now a $500 reward."

The Green Bomber had been sure to up the ante by including the use of plastic explosives near Snow Lake. The mistakes the Forest Service had made included not disclosing the 18 sticks of plastic explosives nor the shotgun shell device placed along the Crest Trail the previous season. Also, the Wilderness Ranger, who was the recipient of the "visitor's" device had failed to get the names of the backpackers. The article also mentioned the "benign" device my partner had tripped. The article also went on to report, "Russell Ray, who has since left his Forest Service job, said…"

My anger had set in motion a full disclosure by the Forest Service. I had met with Gila's main law enforcement officer after receiving a phone call to please come into the supervisor's office. As I couldn't believe that the public wasn't being warned, he let me vent my anger and seemed very interested in the trailhead license numbers I had recorded the previous season. He called the district's information officer into the meeting so they could get all the facts straight. I left the meeting with the belief that the first casualty in any war really is the truth.

People have asked me what side of the fence the bombs came from. I have no idea. A fence is a two-dimensional object. The ranchers insisted it was environmentalists. Environmentalists said it was ranchers. I said it was a nutjob. 1996 would prove to be a very different season. I ran the Fire Pro Crew for Sequoia-Kings Canyon National Park. Flying out of a fire my crew and I had worked for a week solid, the skids of the helicopter clipped the treetops. Everyone said I needed to fill out paperwork for this aviation incident. "What incident?" I asked. "Nothing happened!" Cut to an hour later, and I'm in a swimming pool with my baby girl, thinking about how strange this life could be. Thinking about the Green Bomber no more.

Chapter 1
Barranca Del Cobre, 1987

The Train ride to Chihuahua City after a wild night spent in Juarez proved an opportune time to eat a half tab of acid and marvel at the energy level of the whole event. I encountered some film school students on spring break from someplace back East, and when I commented on the Cecil B. DeMille sunset, they responded, "Who's that?" I retired to another part of the train. As if on some director's cue, the train's electrical wires between two of the cars began to shoot a shower of sparks, illuminating the darkened passageway in an eerie light and providing psychotropic entertainment as the conductors told everyone to stay calm. The sparks seemingly danced to the tune of starting a conflagration, and all efforts were made to staunch the flow of electrons and bring the dance to a conclusion.

The night before had seen my friend Greg and I run drunkenly from a bar after we detected a detective seemingly trying to trip us up in some kind of shakedown scheme that involved us accompanying him on a supposed visit to a donkey show. As Greg exclaimed, "He's a cop," and the suspect amigo unconvincingly tried producing some kind of proof from his wallet to prove he wasn't on the job, I quite clumsily spilled my drink on his laid-out wallet contents. We got up and ran like hell a mile or so back to our hotel room, exclaiming "safe" as we slid into the home plates of our beds. The walk to the train station the next morning had us manifesting like Atomic Spies as we didn't desire repercussions from the previous evening's frivolities. The train ride represented a distancing, a feeling of being safe, as well as being a calming restart to our canyon adventure.

Jody seemed to have the clearest vision of our trip itinerary, as she was the Outdoor Club member who had suggested the trip in the first place, and the group followed her lead in getting off the Juarez train and making our way to the Copper Canyon-bound train. Upon reaching Divisadero, Copper Canyon revealed its magnificent self. The question now was what to do. I shouldered my pack and said that we should follow the road south, skirting along the rim of the canyon until we reached a little village where the sign read "Aeroponapuchi". There was a gap in the fence, and I somehow knew that we needed to descend there. The canyon bottom seemed some thousands of feet down, but onward we went, Jody, her two children, a childhood friend of theirs, Susan, Greg, and myself. We didn't really know what we were getting into.

At one point, the trail started ascending after we had been consistently descending for a few miles, the whole while, it being rather steep. We looked to our left and saw a gentleman off in the distance furiously waving up at us and signaling for us to come down to him. We backtracked to him, where he motioned us to enter his abode. Once inside, he let us know that we had been on the right trail but that he wanted to sell us cold sodas. The cold sodas alleviated the feelings of frustration at this at the first perceived waste of energy. He advised that we should continue back on the trail we had been on, and then we would top out on a rise before descending straight down to the river.

And what a descent it was. The trail bombs down to the Rio Urique to a place with hot springs and huge citrus trees right alongside the Rio Urique. It was like a mini-Paradise. The fragrance of the citrus trees almost masked the smell of formic acid, which served to alert us to the presence of ant members of the family Formicidae. This dictated where we set up to sleep the night at the Canyon bottom. The next day was spent enjoying the beautiful Rio Urique. With its brilliant emerald green color and entrancing ambiance, it was very inviting to get in and cool off in the hot canyon bottom. As we needed to access the beach on the other side of the river, Greg and I utilized a cut bamboo pole to ferry the children across the river, with Jody letting me know that if we drowned her children, Baku and Naphi, along with their friend Mars, she would kill me. The day was so gloriously spent. Women came along to wash clothing in the hot springs, and we helped ourselves to citrus fruits.

The next morning, the need was to ascend the canyon back up to meet the train, as we only had one week of spring break for this outing. The way out was arduous and steep. We watered up really good for the climb out to avoid running out of water. I would hike ahead a few hundred feet and drop my pack to return to piggyback seven-year-old Naphi back up to my backpack, where we would wait for the group to catch up, and then I would repeat this leap-frogging action. We made the top without having run out of water, despite the children insisting they were dying of thirst as they persisted in eating salty snacks.

We were able to catch the return train in Aeroponapuci after finding a tienda where we bought well-deserved cold sodas and snacks.

The return trip was without any extreme antics, and it included a pleasant awakening by the Mexican Military as I slept on the Juarez Train Station floor. They wanted a closer look at a wall mural I was sleeping by. I ended up sleeping on the floor of the train station after an Outward Bound instructor had interloped on my hotel bed while we were out cutting the rug. While in Juarez, Greg, Susan, and I had found a private disco club where the bouncer doorman was more than glad to let us enter once he got a look at beautiful Susan. We danced the night away. We also chalked up this 1987 Western New Mexico Outdoor Club Spring Break trip as a resounding adventure. One for the books.

Chapter 2
Barranca Del Cobre, 1990

The plan was to descend into the Rio Urique via the now-known trail that descends approximately 5,000 vertical feet to the river below the village of Aeroponapuchi, passing down to the river's confluence with the Arroyo Agua Caliente. From there, we would go upriver approximately seven miles to meet up with the Eye of the Canyon trail and then ascend quite arduously to the village of Divisadero a mile up above. We would be able to pick up this untrodden trail by knowing that when we passed the opening of the Eye of the Canyon Arroyo, we would be able to look up and see the Divisadero train stop. We took mini-binoculars to aid in the visualization, just in case.

The "we" on this trip included my wife, Gail, and our mutual friend Jane, who was out of Kansas City, as well as Mark and Pat and Phil and Shelly. Mark and Pat were fellow Silver City, New Mexico, residents, with Mark being an incredible part-time professional photographer, and his wife Pat being an alumnus of New Mexico Tech, where Gail and I had met in college. Phil was a visiting Irishman friend to all, and Shelly was a river guide down from Washington State.

The steep trail down from Aeroponapuchi had everyone schooled in a good understanding of what we were up against. There is nothing like a boots-on-the-ground demonstrative lesson that laid to rest any questions regarding what we were trying to accomplish on this trip. We had driven our Volkswagen van right to the village of Aeroponapuchi, first stopping to camp the night at Pancho Villa State Park. The next morning, we actually needed to tow the van across the border using Mark's truck so he and I could affect a repair on a busted fan bearing which would require the use of a welder. As luck would have it, we secured the use of a home auto repair garage, right across the border in Palomas, Mexico, complete with a welder. Paying for renting the facility and for the Mexican mechanic and his son's help pitching in on the job made the repair feel top-notch. Especially in light of the fact that back home in Silver City, Mark was our mechanic. When the repair was finished, the night was spent in a Mexican border hotel, where Jane had a difficult encounter with an apparently drunk and belligerent Mark. This incident would prove to be a precursor.

The drive to Aeroponapuchi was very uneventful. Cooking dinner in the Volkswagen van while camping on the rim of the Barranca del Cobre seemed to really cement the reality of our proposed adventure. I no longer referred to the canyon as Copper Canyon. I now had a copy of "National Parks of Northwest Mexico" (Richard D. Fisher, 1988) that gave some seemingly useful information on the area. Referencing "Las Barrancas del Cobre" intimated the existence of more than one canyon. There was the Barranca del Cobre, as well as the Barrancas Sinforosa and Batopilas, each containing a sister river of the Rio Fuerte. All too fascinating. I had no real idea of the section of the canyon we intended to ascend. I had no map. It seemed it was sure to prove to be very mysterious. As the book I had contained only sketchy information on this canyon portion, it would definitely be worthwhile to have more of a gander at an unknown expanse of the Rio Urique flowing at the bottom of the Barranca del Cobre.

The heat of the descent had everyone glad to reach the canyon bottom. Once we reached the river bottom, we cooled off in the river and relaxed. The camp was set up, and Mark producing an entire case of beer from his backpack went a long way toward explaining his appearance of being top-heavy and struggling on the way down. The way down had tempers flare about my ability, or inability, to successfully lead this particular trip. I was glad to reach the river, and truth be told, the beers went down well. Decisions needed to be made regarding my feelings about this group I was leading, and a good night's sleep would certainly aid the potentially unpleasant bit of business that needed tending. The canyon at this stretch is so incredibly beautiful, and it lends itself to relaxing and forgetting any woes. All other considerations could wait. It was now just time to revel in being where we were and to contemplate the probabilities of going upriver.

We had no wetsuits nor floating backpacks. We were not as yet "canyoneers". We were backpackers, and as such, we would just have to deal with what was thrown at us. The following morning necessitated a decision that only Gail, Jane, and I would continue upriver. This met with much grumbling, but I expressed the concept of free will. Everyone was free to go up river, but I didn't want any responsibility attached to getting everyone there. We had made it to the river, and that should serve as a goal met. Phil and Shelly both expressed a sincere desire to continue, whereas Mark and Pat did not. I let it be known that it would be all right for Phil and Shelly to accompany us but that they needed to show group solidarity. They agreed, and off we went. It was all for the best, as Mark and Pat were freed up to drink beer and relax on the river as long as they chose, without any trepidation regarding the direction needed to get back home.

The travel upriver was met with a decidedly gentle river stretch, with no big swims or boulder choking encountered and only standard backpacking-type, fairly low river crossings. The Eye of the Canyon was reached, and the Divisadero was plainly visible without the aid of magnification. The trail was right there on the north aspect of the Eye of the Canyon Arroyo. We set up camp and had a very pleasant evening, smoking hashish around the campfire and exchanging lively conversation and laughter. The laughter and the appearance of bioluminescent worms were both accentuated by the hashish. The next morning had us enduring a very long and steep ascent to the top. At one point, Phil expressed displeasure with my ascending like a monkey. I took that to mean I should slow down. When we topped out, the Divisadero was right there, and cold beers were also in close proximity. After many beers, we staggered to Aeroponapuchi to tie in with the van and spend the night.

The next morning saw Phil heading off back to the States and the girls and I deciding to drive to Batopilas. This entailed a retracing to Creel and then a long drive to the dirt road cutoff to Batopilas. The 5,000-foot dirt road descent into Batopilas that followed was alternately exhilarating and terrifying. Two nights spent in Batopilas included a day hike to Satevo. It is an old Spanish Mission church where some unfortunate soul's bones lay in repose up on the altar. The fact that the church was filled with Wasps only added to the ambiance. The need to drive the steep road back up out of the Barranca Batopilas had me suggesting we leave at 4:00 am in order to avoid the Volkswagen van overheating. The girls protested, and a compromise of leaving at 5:00 am was struck. I set the alarm for 3:00 am, and we were on the road by 4:00 am without Gail, Jane, and Shelly being any the wiser.

A coyote trotted in front of the engine-gunning Volkswagen van for mile after mile. Shelly grew testy with my not just stopping to let the coyote go. I pointed out to her that I in no way wanted to lose momentum and that the coyote appeared to be communicating with us as it made its way up the dirt road just fine. The trickster was acting as a kind of mystical guide as we topped out just as the sun was rising. It was as if the coyote was saying, "Come on, just let's go." On the way to camp at Laguna Arareco, the van pooped out. As I repaired a sticking throttle cable, the girls sat on the hillside and glared at me. This served no purpose toward fixing the van, and in my typical fashion, I just silently made the repair, and we were on our way with me harboring resentment.

The camp was so pleasant that I was able to get over it. What proved cosmically impossible to get over was the numerous begging, obviously poor and hungry, Tarahumara Indians who began arriving at our campsite in need of food and money. I started giving all we had, and they kept coming. I finally cried out that I could do no more and shut myself up in the van. What followed was a fitful night's sleep filled with decompressing dreams about potential human conditions. Sadness tugged at my soul. It is a sadness as weighty as any backpack carried while engaging in atavistic frivolity.

Chapter 3
Barranca Del Cobre, 1991

"It is amazing that these incredible chasms have not been documented in the modern era. It took the development of Canyoneering techniques to make these areas accessible to exploration and documentation."

So reads Fisher's book on the Barranca del Cobre area. Just what was canyoneering? Obviously, it meant passing down through canyons, and it must certainly be separate from rafting. Rafting and boating seemed a well-understood and practiced pursuit. To enter a canyon that hadn't been documented in this day and age must certainly be understood to mean that the canyon in question stymies the use of watercraft and that special considerations must come into play when contemplating descending a canyon that hadn't been traditionally traversed. Fisher's book further states:

"The general consensus is that the Barranca del Cobre is unsuitable for any type of traditional river travel. Most, if not all expeditions, to this canyon have not been able to achieve their objectives due to the extreme nature of the river bed terrain, inappropriate techniques, and equipment not suitably adapted to canyon topography. The Barranca del Cobre is made impassable by a huge boulder

pile and waterfalls, which occur approximately ten miles downstream of the Umira bridge. This boulder pile is where the river goes underground for over a mile."

With this information in mind, we set off to descend the Barranca del Cobre from the bridge at Umira all the way to the village of Urique. As for equipment, we would utilize wetsuits, waterproof floating backpacks, rappelling rope and harness, figure eight, a bolt kit, and stout walking sticks made in situ. With all the required food, sleeping and shelter gear, knives, clothing, first aid, maps, altimeter, water bottles, cooking equipment, and personal comfort items, the packs were coming in at an average of 80 pounds each for an estimated two weeks of unresupplied canyon bottom travel. 1:50,000 metric topo maps were purchased in Juarez Mexico at the INEGI (Instituto Nacional de Estadística y Geografía) office.

As far as technique goes, we all knew how to hike, swim, and rappel. I was a wilderness EMT, wildland firefighter, and a member of Search and Rescue, and we could all orienteer to varying degrees. Also to differing degrees were the other party members' personal outdoor experiences and temperaments. Gail and Jane are both accomplished backpackers, and with Gail being a dentist, she had a lot of medical knowledge. Jane was strong and had a great disposition. Dean was a Minnesota country boy with all the requisite outdoorsy life experience that came with it. Scott was my supervisor working for the U.S. Forest Service, and I had ascertained that he should make a strong team member. In other words, we would be flying by the seat of our pants.

The designing of waterproof floating backpacks simply entailed the usage of large river bags strapped to backpacking frames. The wetsuits we chose were the ones designed for windsurfing to not be so stifling to hike in, and you could always peel down the top to accomplish any significant hiking and bouldering required and therefore avoid overheating. As Gail and I were married and living in Silver City, New Mexico, and both Dean and Scott also lived in Silver City, coordinating gear and equipment proved a team effort. With Jane, as she lived out of state, I needed to send explicit instructions to her to guide her on what to bring, and I let it be known that if she were to show up in Mexico with a heavy-duty garbage bag tied to a frame, she wouldn't go on the expedition. After our canyon trip of the previous year, I actually had faith in her to do the right thing. We had trained and competed in Tae Kwon Do together while Gail and I lived in Kansas City, Missouri, so I certainly knew her to be strong.

On the **17th of March, 1991**, the plan was set in motion by first driving to Creel, Mexico, with the battle-tested Volkswagen van and Scott in his truck. As Jane was set to arrive by train, while Gail and the boys situated the van at Aeroponapuchi, I awaited the arrival of the train in Creel in order to meet up with her. We had set up residency at Margarita's the night before. Margarita's is essentially a canyon-bound meeting lodge complete with food and rooms. I had become aware of this accommodation by obtaining the first edition (1989) of M. John Fayhee's book, "Mexico's Copper Canyon Country," as a companion piece to the 1988 Rick Fisher book I already had. John spoke of Margarita's as the place to be. As we were paranoid about not entering the canyon harboring any foodborne illnesses, the decision had been made to cook our own food instead of eating out. Our arrival night had Margarita busting us cooking dinner in the van parked outside her establishment. She was not pleased with my attempts at reasoning the action with her, so for diplomatic considerations, we dropped this plan and had a delicious breakfast at Margarita's the next morning, the morning that dawned on our need to situate the Volkswagen van.

Gail and Jane had agreed to accompany the expedition only to the halfway point, where a climb-out to get them back to the waiting van would occur. They could then make the return trip to New Mexico. Gail was worried and had pleaded with me to heed the words in Fisher's book:

"The Barranca del Cobre is made impassable... Most, if not all expeditions, to this canyon have not been able to achieve their objective due to the extreme nature of the river bed terrain..."

Jane was also convinced of the author's stated wisdom on this matter, whereas Dean, Scott, and I were willing to give the full stretch a goer.

We were able to enter the river canyon bottom by first hitchhiking to the bridge at Umira. The ride on a large flatbed truck had us all excited as we started down the river on a **Monday**. We made our way to the "Incised Meanders," a place well-traveled documented, and photographed. At only a couple of leisurely miles down from the bridge at Umira and at 5,500 feet, our first camp was set up on a nice sandy beach by a great window arch midway along the Meander ridge. This place was incredible, with evidence of high water above where we were camped.

"The Rio must be awesome at that time, literally impassable except for some maniac whitewater person."

—*Russell Ray, from my personal travel journal*

My back was killing me from a lot of pack lifting. I have an old back injury that was getting older. I set a trout line out in hopes of catching fish. There are numerous cypress and ponderosa pines on this segment of the river.

On **Tuesday**, after hiking only 1.5 miles from camp, we had to utilize our wetsuits to swim in a huge pool filled with very cold water. The pool was topped by two waterfalls pouring into it. I got majorly cold as we had to continuously swim and scramble while making our way down through mega-bouldering and big pools. The going never got easy. We were all wishing for more sunshine as we finally made it to the Arroyo Umira, where a warming fire was immediately started. I was shivering quite severely, and less inclement weather would have helped make the water more attractive to motor in. There was a real "scary" component to the day, offset by how spectacular the canyon was.

"All in all, it was a blast. Intense and surreal."

Gail likened it to an acid trip. We hoped to make what we were calling the "hard part" tomorrow. We had covered only approximately four as-the-crow-flies miles of the canyon bottom, but as we don't fly like crows, it felt like and probably was, double that accounting for the side-to-side, up-and-down undulating path forced upon us.

"3/20/91 Weds. 12:45 pm

Approx. three miles from the A.U. confluence & we are hunkered in an overhang with a fire roaring! This place is spectacular. The 1st 1.5 miles was fairly easy. Now it is Boulder Field City. Since for the third day in a row, it is overcast/raining the agua part tends to be chilly—hence the fire. We may not go much further today (?). We should be at the "hard part" soon if we aren't already! We warm Oatmeal/fire/snacks I feel warmed. Jane is having trouble with her feet (numb). Dean suggests we stay here and try out this new pipe I made out of Bamboo— Tonight around the fire! The Rio is moving due North, almost directly, so we have a good idea of our location."

Thursday morning had us waking up in camp at an old Tarahumara dwelling/goat pen, approximately five miles from the Arroyo Umira confluence. Once again, the difficulty of the terrain passage had us only completing a little greater than five canyon miles to get there. We needed to stop for a warming fire on the way after some serious swimming coupled with rain and a decided lack of sunshine. The day had at first manifested clear blue after a night with the sky pulsating a blaze of a billion bright stars. We were somewhere into the west bend the Rio takes above the long north stretch encountered after passing the Arroyo Umira. The altimeter read 4,900 feet.

As Dean rolls a ciggy, Scott repairs his boots, Gail makes coffee, Jane is Jane, and I write in my journal. As the day is clear, we are psyched on this, the first day of spring. What a gorgeous day as we pushed 1.5 miles to reach the confluence with the Arroyo Basihuare. Though the going is tough and intense, it is not lost on us how incredible this place really is. All of the team members are likewise incredible. Sometimes, I get too intense to perceive myself as being incredible. We are committed at this point, and despite me having a swollen ankle caused by wiping out three times two days ago, it is always just time to go, go, go.

The camp was pitched just past the Vado north up Arroyo Aboreachi, and to the south, it exits up to La Dominga. The altimeter seems to confirm this. Canyoneering is a series of contour line crossings, and periodically the altimeter must be reset. Dead reckoning is always in play to help assure accurate map placements. The Arroyo Aboreachi is an amazing slot canyon bombing right off the ridge, with the map indicating the dubious existence of a trail. The day involved numerous swims, with one box swim approximating 500 feet, plus another large one, and numerous other pools and rapids. Jane got dangerously cold, and we needed to start a large warming fire.

Friday, the second day of spring, we had reached another large meander. The river is dropping rather swiftly in through here. The backsides of meanders always present huge boulders to contend with, as that is where the dissipating energy deposits them. What a meander it was. It nearly tapped us out. Lots of big bouldering and swimming, and crossing to avoid swimming.

"We stopped today after some impressive trucking. While we weren't cold, we had just finished an exceptionally long swim, and we were faced with another. We set up camp on this excellent beach with a wall fireplace, lots of dry wood, and a lot of pretty Mountain Cottonwoods! There is a classic C.C. view (photographed roll #3) just off the beach which fronts our property. This basically is the backside of the Meander. If the water were to come up, we can escape up on the wall! Excellent spot! Cont. This place is most Tropical in appeal with Fig Trees and various Agave types hanging from the Canyon walls. The water is Emerald and reflects the intense green of some lush-looking Plant that is growing in a seep close to the bank. Jane is having trouble with her feet, and it does slow things down, but the pace is logical and sustainable. Jane is a champ. Gail is incredibly tough, and after getting her feet (and stuff) wet, she is a strong member and doesn't complain! Scott is amazing! Dean is amazing! This whole experience is amazing! We hope to make El Tejeban takeout tomorrow and think about a day off! Five days out/amazing!"

In lieu of **Saturday** morning cartoons, we passed through the antiquated gold mining pueblo of Barranca del Cobre, the place where a trail exits to both El Tejeban and Huancayo. We were able to converse with two Mexican miners. After 76-year-old Manuel Ramirez boulder-traversed using a wooden plank over to us, we took a descanso. Dean rolled Manuel a cigarette, and we shot the shit. These were the ruins of a once-prosperous mining operation. A dilapidated hacienda perched over the

Rio Urique that was experiencing a pronounced color change as it flowed past the mine. Arrastras and amalgamation made the water suspect. We pushed on to camp shy of the Arroyo Bachutare. This place was both majestic and by far the widest part of the canyon yet seen.

"Actually, we passed into a little narrower part downriver from a very wide spot (with houses) by swimming an epic swim—the longest yet, by far! The water is turning back to its same Emerald color/clear. The huge pool we swam in must act as a settling pool. Fish are jumping."

The water had now cleared, and the canyon wall towered to our right. Downriver could be seen where the Arroyo Bachutare meets the Rio Urique, and there the canyon starts its great bend to the southwest. We hoped to reach the Rio Cusarare the next day. We had plenty of time to make the takeout at Arroyo Ojo Caliente. The potential was there to finally have a rest day. As the canyon had really opened up, tremendous views were afforded. Although we prudently anticipated upcoming tough spots, we were feeling very confident after spending five days passing through the upper Barranca del Cobre, the most incredible wilderness experience of my life. Little black-biting batards were becoming a nuisance, but being famished and exhausted made their appearance of scant concern. Plus, Avon Skin So Soft had a pronounced effect on them.

Sunday had us reach the Rio Cusarare. Though a large drainage, not much water flowed out of it. Our bearings had been thrown by passing an unexpected high water-flowing arroyo that came in from our left. It had as much, if not more, water flowing from it than any arroyo we had yet encountered. After leaving camp, a large swim was required through a box with a suspension bridge over it. As the day was hot, the swimming proved enjoyable, and the going was fast and relatively easy. After putting in a long hard day, on this, our 7th day out, we covered 5+ river miles. Here, at this campsite that is somewhere shy of the Arroyo San Ignacio (Tararecua Canyon), exists a beautiful waterfall coming into the Urique. As the "Rio" Cusarare was not only an anticlimax, it had really thrown our navigation.

"We were thrown on our orienteering today. Scott is so dedicated to this pursuit and is quite good. I guess I'm not so dedicated. We all participate in the maps to one extent or another, some more than others (I carry them!). What a day! The rock wall against which is the fire is blowing shrapnel rock out with loud reports. The Moscos are out and commencing to slash! Gail goes through her food. I love her! I should think about our sleeping arrangements about now. We will hike hard again mañana, and then maybe earn a rest day finally, we shall see!"

Monday, the first of our usual two lunch stops had us approaching the meander loop where the Tararecua Canyon spills the Arroyo San Ignacio into the Rio Urique. As the sun was blazing, no wetsuits were required. It felt glorious to have started the day with a leisurely breakfast and a couple of cups of coffee. Swimming is now enjoyable and required for cooling off.

"We are situated at the mouth of Tararecua / Arroyo San Ignacio. What a day! Our reckoning was off in that we were too optimistic about our distance traveled. Now we can have our bearings once again and start down River in a familiar part of the Canyon (G., J., R. that is!). While it is true that the Canyon opens up at La Mina Barranca del Cobre, it is not true that you are always moving through this "open" Canyon at that much faster pace! We are busting our asses, and we are covering the distances desired (longer!) Tomorrow we may make the Areponapuchi / A. Ojo Caliente trailhead, but I'm not willing to die for it! He says!!!"

As we spiked out on the beach at the Divisadero's "Eye of the Canyon" trail, **Tuesday** had us making the decision to hike with the girls out here instead of at the Arroyo Agua Caliente. This was pretty much a "because it's there" decision that both Gail and Jane really advocated for. Dean and I would go with the girls up, and as it was feasible, we could buy some corn tortillas, cheese, jalapeños, and more booze. Scott would continue down the canyon to wait for us at the Arroyo Caliente. I didn't mind foregoing this canyon section down to the Arroyo Agua Caliente as I had just done it the year before, and though gorgeous, it wasn't really canyoneering.

As we had passed the mouth of Tararecua Canyon at 11:45, this meant we could generate a half day to relax before climbing out the following day. The going encountered was not easy sailing, and while traversing a wall above a long box filled with very cold water that I had grown loath to get in, I managed to swan-dive approximately 40 feet into the water below, pack and all. A spider, seemingly the size of my hand, had climbed on top of my gripping hand. In a nanosecond, it had afforded me a relative size comparison. I seemed to peel so fast as to move backward in time to a point where the spider hadn't actually scuttled on top of my hand at all. After my pack and I splashed down, I resurfaced, cursing up at the offending arachnid. At that moment in time, I truncated a fear of falling with arachnophobia, and I'm really not afraid of spiders. Falling, however, I can do without.

On **Wednesday**, it took us 7.5 hours to top out at Divisadero. We overclimbed as we so obviously hadn't followed the same exact trail as the previous year. Equally steep, this trail led us to a point looking down 100 feet at the Divisadero train station and the source of cold beers. The way up is killer, plain and simple. I don't recommend it for canyon ingress nor egress.

After drinking many beers, we staggered a couple of miles from Aeroponapuchi to the Tarahumara Mission Hotel. There we could get dinner, and equally important, more beers. A caveat also being that Aeroponapuchi is where the van was parked, and if we could score hotel rooms, we would be really set. Dean and I planned on descending the following day after the girls were off. Beers taste so good when you earn them. Even when you don't earn them. Dinner was so excellent, and there was plenty of lively conversation as there were loads of Germans staying at the inn. We retired to sitting by the fire, awaiting word on a room. Sadly, a room didn't pan out, but the manager, Maria, consented to let us rack out on the floor of the dining hall. As this great room had a large roaring fire, it seemed like a good alternative to spiking out, though hot showers would be missed. The Germans finally got their drunken asses off to bed, and we got to get all comfy. Gail mistook Dean's snoring for me offering bedtime offense, and chucked a shoe at me. How reactively mistaken and precious of her.

The following day after making our tienda purchases and seeing the girls off, it took us five hours to descend to the Rio Urique down the Aeroponapuchi trail. Upon reaching the Warm Springs River bottom, a multitude of campers greeted our arrival. Not seeing Scott, we moved down river ¼ mile. It was Easter and hence vacation time. One person we spoke with indicated that Scott had passed through. Due to Scott's nature, that made a lot of sense, as he would want to distance the hoards. This part of the canyon was very open. The night was spent amongst huge boulders as a very full moon made it appear almost like daytime with all the light-colored boulders acting like giant reflectors. It made sleeping difficult having a huge nightlight in the sky turning the canyon bottom into a surreal landscape.

Thursday night proved chilly as the canyon must experience a lot of cold air drainage. It was looking like it would take two days to reach the Arroyo Hondo, the end of the Barranca del Cobre, and the beginning of the Barranca Urique. After that, it should be one plus days to the village of Urique. **Friday** had us make good progress in our effort to reach the Arroyo Hondo after tying in with Scott a short distance down the canyon. Scott was encountered lounging on top of a huge boulder serving as a Crow's Nest. The plan was to reach the Arroyo Hondo the next day. We feasted on quesadillas made over the fire using the tortillas, cheese, and jalapeños, and a piece of airplane fuselage wreckage fashioned into a griddle. As we camped, a Tarahumara girl kept checking us out from the opposite bank where she was tending a very large flock of goats.

"Fri. 3/29/91

It took us five hrs to descend to the Urique down the Aeroponapuchi trail. We bee-lined straight down on a well-worn/traveled trail with the need for one little backtrack at the end. We bouldered/swam down approx. ¼ mi. down from the trailhead due to a multitude of campers situated there (approx. 25!). It is Easter and hence vacation time! We heard #'s voices coming from the warm springs. There were approx. a doz. hikers heading out / down. One Gentleman seemed to have spoken to Scott and indicated his movement down the river. A Mexican camper (young boy) seemed to also confirm this. This makes sense due to Scott's nature and the hoards. We are assuming he is down from us, and we will walk toward him & he will hopefully stay put or walk toward us! It is bright and sunny, and we are ahead of schedule for this last leg of the journey. It is a mellow morning, and my legs appreciate it! I love you Gail and cherish your soul. If you were to cast me off, sometimes I wouldn't blame you. I need you for what I lack. I lack a lot. Our lives can be so hurried. You are such a good person. If we fight, I am stupid! Cont. / 4:50 We are camped just down from the Arroyo De La Laja. We put in some miles. At this pace, we may be in Urique on the 1st of April, Mon.! Dean is off exploring. He is so dedicated. I called stop today when a big blister formed on my little toe. Gad zooks, it hurt. Dean was ready to charge on since we had just figged up approx. 10 mins. earlier. Now he is off photoaging. This part of the Canyon is very opened. It does close down but we have seen many settlements in large bench areas. We also noted a lot of no people. We dealt with a lot of young Bulls today. We observed one entering an old dwelling. We passed, and he stared out at us. A bunch of Coatis sauntered by!"

Chilly nights in the canyon are spent with the silence of thoughts that threaten a cacophony of what the brain desires to shed. I endure the cold as the moments in between wakefulness and sleep affords a warm dream world that the psyche longs to crawl back into. I don't deal well with the cold as others do, I only deal well enough. Cold nights, cold water, they can be survived. They can be transcended. We awake to a world not benign and get up and go. We revel in life given us to live beyond the confines of subjectivity. The objective world will nudge your corpse with its toes and exclaim, "Yeah, he's dead!" Thoughts of how badly humans can suffer in the earthly plain place relativity to all current actions. Jane had suffered so from the cold, and I dreamed that Gail and she were safe and warm.

"Sat. 3/30/91 cont. 5:20 pm
We have made it halfway to A. Hondo as planned, but what an effort. A lot of bouldering and big swims against the wind! In the last big box, there was wave action and even some "Ocean Spray" action. It was, needless to say, exhausting. There appears to be a cable or power line across from our spectacular camp. It is partway up a little drainage and spans

the Arroyo! Up River, a couple of hundred feet and across is a little waterfall entering the Urique River. We will have some of Gail's Chili tonight. I miss her, and I think about her. I hope the trip home is w/o incident. She is my tough/strong love."

Easter Sunday dawned without clouds. The very bright moon had created an effect of snow-capped peaks in the night. Approaching the Arroyo Hondo, we realized by studying the maps that the canyon would be intense. This proved to be accurate, as this section of canyon rivaled the upper Barranca del Cobre in difficulty. We passed through what might be the tightest section of canyon there is. We also swam through a box approaching 600 feet in length. It was definitely Wetsuit City with the need to swim, swim, swim.

While setting up a well-deserved camp, Dean shook a 1-inch scorpion from his river bag. Apparently, it was a celestial canyon hitchhiker. More like a Supertramp that I flicked off our bench camp. The river takes a substantial bend here, quite visible from our camp. Today we had been approached by three Tarahumara children who made contact, with the older sister shaking our hands in turn. She had a sweet smile, and I gave her and her sister colorful bandanas. I gave a pocket knife to the little brother. The older sister spoke Spanish with me but was too shy to tell me her name. She was learning Spanish in school, and as they were on their way to church, they donned their new bandanas, and with smiles, they were off.

Upon reaching the Arroyo Hondo, we found it had a substantial volume of water flow. Sitting around our confluence camp, we toasted cheers with some relished El Presidente brandy and smoked a bowl. While contemplating the universe, sitting by the fire feeling no pain, a large toad hopped over into plain view. Seemingly looking us over, it hopped right into the fire and roasted itself to our amazed horror. Despite this bordering on a portentous occurrence, which brought to mind the Vietnam-era Buddhist monk, we realized how fortunate we were to be so deep into this beautiful canyon.

"Mon. 4/1/91 8:15 pm I write this dead tired and drunk in our Hotel room at "Hotel Canyon" in Urique! We busted ass and put in our biggest day to get here today at 6:00 pm."

While it is true that Urique is a dry town, it is also true that you could buy cold caguamas of beer wrapped in newspaper. The Hotel Canyon had plenty of hot water for showers, and the restaurant Zuelma was right next door. There the food was excellent, and you could buy beer. The proprietor surmised that we were from New Mexico based on how we ate the spicy hot food. A road had been cut down to the village the year before, as evidenced by numerous trucks and other vehicles. We would be able to secure a ride to the train station up top at Bahuichivo for $6.50. Up top being 6,000 vertical feet away. The village was incredibly quaint, and the people were very friendly. Urique was certainly more alluring than Batopilas.

Alas, we decided to shoulder our packs and hike out of town in order to hitch a ride further up the road. A wrong turn had us ending up at the village dump, where we plopped down in the heat. We proceeded to eat acid and hang out and drink our cold newspaper-wrapped beers. We had a commanding Movietone view of the village. Eventually, a horseback rider showed up to inquire just what in the fuck we were doing. We told him we had taken a wrong turn but that we would return to town to spend the night. Back in the village, they refused to sell us more beer, and we ended up spiking out on the beach for the night.

The next morning, we paid the fare for a ride to the train station and made our way to Creel to spend the night at Margarita's and retrieve Scott's truck. The road out of Urique is very reminiscent of the spectacular Batopilas road. The trip home was uneventful until we reached the U.S. Border, where, despite our telling them we worked for the U.S. Forest Service they decided to put us through the drill. Remembering I had a tab of acid in my front shirt pocket, I attempted to slyly fish it out to flick it away. I dropped it on the front seat just as they wanted Sparky the Wonder Dog to give the truck cab a good sniffing. I felt sure the dog would hoover the hit up its snoot and that we should consider hanging for the Spark Show. They sent us on our way. I found the LSD Tab on the seat, and I repocketed it.

"Thurs. 4/4/91 7:20 am

Today, we head home. Since we have approx. 500 miles to drive, we will probably drive straight through and get to Silver City this evening! With this Journal, I have neglected to mention every little and big event. It is hardly possible to write about all the grandeur we have seen. We can hope for several pictures that will approximate the feel of the Canyon, but as always, it will live on most vividly in our minds! To me, the upper part of Barranca del Cobre is the best but is closely rivaled by the stretch above and below the Arroyo Hondo. On the last day in the Canyon, we needed wetsuits and accomplished the longest swim of the expedition. We spotted an Amphitheater there, which is the grandest I've yet seen and is a place I would love to return to someday. We talk now about Barranca Sinforosa sometime soon. Right now, my knee isn't talking any such thing. Maybe in a year. It is possible to descend the Barranca del Cobre w/o resupply in approximately two wks. time. If this is done, expect very heavy packs at the Bridge near Umira and expect long hard days, every day!"

Chapter 4
Barranca Sinforosa, 1992

The sense of accomplishment that came with having descended the Barranca del Cobre the year before had us feeling a high level of confidence that we could do likewise and succeed on the Barranca Sinforosa. The previous year's expedition to the Barranca del Cobre had me self-deluded that we had actually pulled off the first descent, but shortly after returning home, I learned of the great Dick Griffith's 1952 two-stage first descent of the Barranca del Cobre that he accomplished along with his wife, Isabelle Galo Griffith. He accomplished this six years before I was even born. I also learned of Don Mattox's 1975 full descent of the Barranca del Cobre, this occurring the year before I graduated high school. The Fisher book I had on the Barrancas could potentially have expounded on these previous efforts, as people apparently were very well aware of Dick Griffith's 1952 successful canyon descent. While I was not aware, truth be told, I didn't need any book to explain the feeling that I had that there was no way we could have been the first, and we certainly wouldn't be the last, to pass through the great Barranca del Cobre. With the Sinforosa, I just went with the feeling that ours would be the first descent, as I hadn't been led to believe any differently. As there was no "road map," what we did have were the numerous 1:50,000 metric topo maps required to paint a picture that would help guide us.

We made the Rio Verde on **Tuesday, the 3rd of March, 1992**. With this expedition, there were seven of us. Dean, Scott, and I had been joined by Dave, Shelly, Tom, and Boscoe the Wonder Dog. Dean and Scott, both being seasoned at this point, had been instrumental with the decision to include unknowns into the mix. Shelly had been along on the 1990 upriver Barranca del Cobre trip, where she comported herself very well, so I vouched for her. And as fate would have it, Dave and Shelly were both river guides out of Washington State. That level of experience should certainly prove beneficial to this effort. Tom was an acquaintance from Silver City who, upon learning of our trip plans, had approached me with a desire to be included.

The trip down into Mexico had us all jam-packed into Dave's large pickup truck. I had to forge the required paperwork for the truck in order to get it into Mexico. The forgery looked so real after a notary friend put her stamp on it. The "us" all jam-packed into the truck included the seven expedition members along with Jody, her daughter Naphi (both from the 1987 Barranca del Cobre trip!), and Rex. The three extras along were there to drive the truck back to the U.S. from our San Carlos drop-off on the rim of the Barranca Sinforosa.

The rim would prove a genesis of sorts. It is where early fracturing began. It started with a heated discussion over money outlay, with everybody wanting an accounting right then and there. I grew angry as I had been shouldering most of the financial burden. Rex, the math professor, refused to chime in with any accounting advice. I came up with a system that had money being physically given out and then needing to be physically given back to me. It was demonstrative Accounting

101. I ended up with all the money, and the others (excluding Dean and Scott) grumbled about being broke. I just mentally said, "Fuck you," as my spirit was so saddened. I hadn't wanted to be concerned about economic pragmatics. I felt like all considerations beyond descending the Barranca Sinforosa could wait. Another bone of contention had been the hiring of a guide, something we had never done before, as we were explorers. But Dave and Shelly had insisted. That expenditure I had to meet as I had all the money at that point. When we ended up being "guided" 1.5 days above where we really wanted to enter the canyon bottom, the fractured die was really cast. Having Jody and Shelly give me hugs after the great money debacle went a long way toward resetting my spiritual compass bearing.

"I awoke at 5:00 am to rain. I had been awakened several times to this sound. It was hard to actually be motivated. I had to set an example. When I stepped out onto the porch, it was a real downpour. Everyone eventually staggered out. Dave wasn't too thrilled with the prospect of dropping in the rain. We had contracted with Federico the day before, and we were to meet him at 8:00 am. The walk was steep with our full packs—rain!"

On the way down, we had walked through intermittent rain, which we had awoken to as a torrent at 5:00 am. A very gracious family had put all seven of us up for the evening as they seemed genuinely fascinated by what we were attempting. Also, we compensated them for their kind hospitality. Federico the Guide ended up staying with us the first night on the river before heading out in the morning back up to San Carlos. He reports that this stretch of the canyon is known as Barranca de San Carlos and that the Barranca Sinforosa was "mas abajo". It was very steep descending, and at first, we had entered an arroyo (A. Bacureamache) before climbing out and finally descending down to the Rio Verde. On the way down, my not consuming any breakfast calories caught up with me and my very heavy pack. Shelly gave me a PowerBar, and I was able to get my sea legs back again and make it to the river.

"My legs just did not want to carry the weight of the pack and me anymore. They acted like they wanted to buckle, with trembles and all. What a drag. A FIRST, and hopefully last—for this trip at least!"

Wednesday was our first day on the river, and the morning had revealed clear skies. I paid Federico $25.00, as well as giving him a fairly new pair of blue jeans. The rest of the group also ponied up other items to lavish on him. He bundled the booty up in his camping blanket, and he bid us adieu. Almost immediately, we did a perfunctory sans-wetsuit first swim in very cold water. Shivering after the swim saw wetsuit usage become all the rage. Everyone seemed very psyched. Coming upon a drainage and thinking that we had reached the confluence with the Turuachi, our originally desired canyon entry point, had us schooled in disappointment. The Turuachi comes with the header "Rio," and there was no water flowing from this unknown arroyo that we set up camp across from. Upon further study of the map, Scott pronounced we had to be at the Turuachi. The canyon was stunning regardless of our location in it. I made an attempt at the altimeter, getting a reading of 5,175 feet. This didn't correspond with the map, but we just let it go as it was time to relax after our first day of canyoneering. The campsite was by a Tarahumara chili patch, and sampling revealed them to be a quite spicy addition to dinner. That night Tom elected to a spike in the chili patch enclosure.

"Today was fairly easy (terrain) with a lot of ground covered. There were the usual extremes, and it was incredibly beautiful. Cont. Dinner was very tasty courtesy of S.&D. I stretch out, and it felt good. The River is so peaceful. The air feels alive with the River and the Birds. It is amazing how it feels to simplify your life so much. It isn't taking long for the Copper Canyon feeling to seep in. I still have fears (as always) but no bad mishaps to anyone thus far on our 2nd day of major ass busting in this Canyon. This is the best time. The time to feel anabolic. Unlike so much of my life. Cont. A Tara. man just passed upriver from us on the opposite bank. He headed up what we figure is the Rio Turuachi. He was dressed traditionally. He wore a hat and was motoring up the trail quite fast while carrying a red bag in one hand. We waved, but there was no response, although he kept glancing over at us. They probably don't want us here. Oh well, we have to be better than the fat slob we saw riding a small Horse down into the Canyon yesterday!"

Thursday was a glorious third day in the canyon that had dawned sunny. It was as if to announce that having patience with a night that had seen heavy dew and frost would soon yield to a great day of canyoneering. Positive thoughts go a long way toward negating the obvious pitfalls of having a glass half full. My body felt beat up as I awoke sore in my legs and clavicles, but my spiritual outlook was quite good. I so truly believed we were actually a strong group capable of getting this descent done. The nuts and bolts of any arduous activities necessitate the putting away of what is superfluous. Too much weight attached to essentially meaningless distractions is what causes gravitational spins of the mind that can weigh you down. It was better to just forget the angst of the rim.

"Cont. WRONG—We are now at the Rio Turuachi (#3). It is almost equal in volume to the Verde. We were 1 ½ days upriver to start since it is 12:00 now that we are here"

Now we could reset our minds, our orientation, and our expectations. The altimeter could be recalibrated. Though disappointing to have been so far above the Rio Turuachi, to begin with, it had us realizing that we wouldn't want to unsee what we had seen, as it was all too enchanting to have missed. There was a stone arch above the dry faux Rio Turuachi that is the stuff of beauty.

"The terrain is relatively easy, and I can avoid swimming. S. & D. trip along in the agua almost constantly. Cont. We passed into a different Canyon down from the confluence with the Rio T. the bottom becomes very boulder choked with large rocks very similar to our favorite Canyon. We are truly in a big Canyon now, a Barranca. At this spot, the walls (4) tower hundreds of feet. A small waterfall cascades 200 ft. across the stream from

me. We envision staying here forever someday. It would be an excellent place to stash at the end of things the way we know it. Also a great place to guide trips. The Taras absolutely will not deal with us. We saw two women converging on separate trails toward each other. They didn't acknowledge us or each other."

Friday the 6th had us waking up in the best camp ever. The beach and the cascade were a great accompaniment to hot tea and good conversation. Just down from our camp beckoned the 1,400-meter contour line, and if we really humped it, we could make it all the way to the 1,300-meter line. That way, if we were to pass the Arroyo Hondo, we would be back on schedule. Alas, as this camp was so spectacular, it proved hard for the group to motivate.

"This reach of Canyon is simply spectacular with huge rock Palisades and cliff faces. Just down from the A. Bacureamache should be the A. San Carlos. These being approx. 1/4 mi. apart from and both on the N. The A.B. is a large drainage we passed across on our way down to the Verde on our 1st day out. Federico called it A. Rancho. We should pass several settlements today. One is called Satevo. Cont. 4650 ft. at (4) the A. San Carlos. We passed the A. Bacureamache—the Arroyo that we crossed on the way down. This Arroyo approx. ⅛ mi. From the A.B.! We sit and eat lunch, and I realize that we are not making a very good time. We need to push on soon. We need to get earlier starts. We smoke a bowl now. Oh well!"

We camped just down from the Arroyo Del Durazno, with

I doubt that the others noticed a quiet Scott being even more quiescent. That night, I felt I should sleep, but Scott and his pack spending time underwater had made a big impression on me. I missed my wife, Gail. The group alternately appeared as tired and strong, with the subtleties of fracturing strain beginning to show.

Sunday finally saw us pass the 1,300-meter line to reach the Arroyo Napuchis, with an accompanying vision of grandeur that we might also make the 1,200-meter contour line.

"The weather turned clear after I went to bed. I was able to lie and watch the stars. It is cloudless this morning. No large equipment failure for anyone—we all have water leakage, but like bilge water in a boat, it is totally manageable. My shoes are showing wearing."

We had passed a large bowl cut into the north rim that the map clearly showed to get to camp no. 6. It is hot in camp, which is fine with me after all the swimming we did today. At one point, I got seriously fucked up cold.

"Today, we passed a few Tara. Dwellings and saw some Tara. Children and heard their dogs barking. We even came upon laundry laid out to dry w/o the attendant. We came upon an old Marijuana plantation, and Dean harvested. It made me uneasy to come upon. The precedent, I guess. We need to stay out of trouble if possible. We marked the plantation with P.P. at the mouth of a drainage."

My feet and legs were feeling the effort today as we covered approximately 6 miles. Looking at the map had us thinking we were back on schedule for a Santa Ana takeout. Dean lost his pack today in the rapids. His yells at me opened a frame of mind required for me to react quick enough to shed my pack and time a jump into the rapids to snag his pack. This being all well and good, as my pack was now on the other side of some big water with Tom and Scott. I signaled them to wait and that I would cross to them. This proved impossible for me as I kept getting swept off my feet. Dean crossed at a reasonable spot to get my pack, and all was right in the universe. Dean and I met up to exchange packs. The river has really increased in volume after the addition of the Rio Turuachi and other inflows. Finally, there was no dew in the night, but a downside was becoming the sand storms as the down-canyon winds had really kicked up. Shelly was in need of repairing her new hiking boots as the water proves so hard on equipment. The cold water coupled with the wind, made for a very harsh day. It was Sand Blast City while being wet. We swam a huge box with an actual wind wave chop. The rock walls are incredible, adding an aesthetic ambiance hard to ignore. The cold still creeps in every night.

Monday dawned clear and clockwork, marking one solid week of pushing in the Barranca Sinforosa. The 1.5-day start above the Rio Turuachi, along with initial late start days, had jeopardized the master plan of a takeout at Santa Ana. The thinking had been to end with a scoot up and over into the village of Batopilas. As this possibility included a non-canyoning stretch of this barranca, in speaking with Dean and Scott, the consensus was beginning to become a takeout at Guerachi.

I was really beginning to like this plan as I had dropped the denial of my having colitis. The bleeding and frequent bowel movements, beyond being a literal pain in the ass, endangered not only myself but also the group. We were faced with the possibility of running out of food, and if we couldn't resupply in Guerachi, it would become game over by default anyhow.

Today was a long-distance day of trying to make up for the lost time. We saw numerous Tarahumaras and encountered a gravesite and the abandoned village of Reteaporaci. The Tarahumara alerted themselves to us, and us to them utilizing drumming. A small and unoccupied Tarahumara dwelling contained a giant oya, matate, and discarded corncobs. The old fire pit spoke of fairly recent usage. We encountered several marijuana fields, with one of particular note being in Paraje Chinamachi. A commonality all the plantations shared, beyond being destroyed, was the use of black plastic piping set to import side arroyo water sources. The piping had all been destroyed and served as an ominous sign of concern to us. That concern was eventually overcome by the harvesting of pioneer plants. Dave showed a real zeal for the budded plants we encountered. A quick-dry by the campfire with the tasty buds spread out on flat rocks yielded Sinforosa Sensi to die for. Dinner was a lot of food for big appetites that were exacerbated by the munchies. Seven days of hard slogging had us deserving what the canyon would offer. We took all the canyon would give, and "Bring it on" was met by it being brought. The physicality of it all was mercifully tempered by grandeur unparalleled.

"I looked down, and little budded guys were all around. A

quick-dry at dinner and we could partake of Sinforosa Sensi. This went over well with the N.M. chili I served up. A lot of food for big appetites. On this our 7th day, we covered nine mi. In two days, we may be in Paraje Sinforosa. Everyone is very strong now. We take on what the River gives. It feels good."

Tuesday had me being the first one up in the morning, so I got the fire going and put the breakfast water to boil. This being a ritual, and for the most part, everyone is into it. Some more than others. The trip was going parallel to what was planned. At least my legs were holding up as I did have undenied colitis to contend with. So far, it was manageable. I missed Gail. I missed home. The fire's smoke always seems to seek out your face no matter where you sit or stand. It was once again cloudless, on this, our 8th day out.

We hoped to make it through two close contour lines today. Close contour lines usually assure exciting times to be had by all. The altimeter read 3,850 feet. This has been quite the Tarahumara part of the canyon. We heard a lot of drumming. Two young men exited the canyon across from us and proceeded upriver. We saw a little boy and girl and their dog about sundown. We chanced upon some boys playing. The older one was roping and dragging the younger two across the sand. I asked the older boy if he spoke Spanish. He just looked bewildered, and we went on our way. At this point, quite the crowd gathered on the hill to watch us pass. Later, an older couple watched in amazement as we crossed the river.

Clouds rolled in today. It didn't seem to matter, for the day was already strange, overcast, and with a lot of Tarahumaras so reticent with our arrival. I know this was beginning to bother Tom, as he felt we shouldn't even be here. We camped just across the river from where the trail ascends to Guachochi. The A. Guachochi was roaring with water. It was hard to cross. Now the river volume had really increased. I was just too tired in my spirit to take many photos. We were fractured, with a lot of trouble focusing. We inadvertently traipsed across some garden plots and were given the high sign to just keep going by a Tarahumara girl. After much lackadaisical behavior, especially at lunchtime, we ended up putting in a good day distance-wise. We more than covered the distance between the 1,100-meter and 1,000-meter contour lines. Everyone was tired. Dave said that Shelly was crying all the time. Her back was hurting, and she was approaching exhaustion. I gave her Motrin and Percocet. She seemed to do better with the medication regime. I counseled Dave that as Rochelle was his girlfriend, he really needed to be the one to comfort her. In other words, "Just deal with it."

Tom and I engaged in a lively and unpleasant discussion about me not publishing anything regarding this trip. He was obviously feeling guilty over our presence here amongst the Tarahumara and didn't desire a letting on of where they had sought refuge. The truth is, they have always been here. Even more so after the arrival of the Spanish. My feelings were that we were just passing through, and as long as the arrows didn't start flying, we would just be on our way. I meant the Tarahumaras no disrespect, nor did I want to disturb them by just simply passing through, but passing through was the stated purpose of this expedition. This was not anthropological for me, it was topographical. It was putting one boot over the other. The plight of Native people bothers the shit out of me, but here they seem to be holding their traditional own. We didn't bribe them for photo ops, nor did we covet their treasures. Several times Tarahumara drumming was heard, apparently spreading the word of our presence. It seemed to me as a comforting acknowledgment of each other's existence.

Wednesday was another day in the thick of this canyon sojourn. I got swept big-time crossing to our campsite. The increased river volume provides for hours of entertainment. The algae slicking of the river rocks makes for a Canyon on Ice Show that requires care whenever you just don't feel like swimming.

"I got swept big-time crossing to our campsite. With the addition of the A. Guachochi, the Verde is again a fairly big River. I was able to wedge along for ⅔ of the x-ing, but there was one last swift deep channel. I committed, made the boulder I aimed for, but it was slicked with Algae, and away I went. I then trashed like a wildman to eddie-out and thank my lucky stars. Cont. Today is our 9th day out. It seems forever, it seems a short time. We should make Paraje Sinforosa today and possibly more. People want a day off. It would be nice, but in light of our lagging situation, it would be quite a luxury. High, thin clouds this morning. Like yesterday. We are close to 3,000 ft., w/o clouds it would be hot. No wind so far. That seems to be one very irritating and hard to handle factor. As always. It's psychological. I slept very good last nite and seemed to be in synch with it. Cont. We passed the site of Paraje Sinforosa.

Today was a short intense day. We have stopped at ½ day for a little R&R. We all need it, but not all seem to appreciate it. S. & D. are big fans of it. We are close to ½ of our food being gone w/o ½ of the Canyon being done. The doubts grow about the Santa Ana takeout. We can only do what we do. The reality stands. We now have high hopes for Guerachi—food especially. This could extend our time out. It could make it a goer! Cont. It seems I don't seem to care anymore about goals. I say this sincerely, not just related to the factors. Being the leader grows tiresome. It is a good group, but we all need leadership. I'm not particularly even suited for it. But alas. Scott makes dinner in this our 9th camp. Lentils—lots of them hopefully, I'm starved. We are camped by a nice overhang for S&D. Dean is off separate and had been seemingly miffed. He is a good strong (very!) friend."

Thursday would be a day of penance, as the day before, I had to lay it down for everyone (except for Dean and Scott, and especially for Dave and Shelly). We needed to put in three hard days to make Guerachi and not have to climb out there. Three days of arduous effort and procuring more food could assure us of the feasibility of going on. If buying more food ended up being a possibility, that would remove the caloric pressure. I actually broached that Dave and Shelly should exit the canyon, regardless, as that seemed to be for the best. I got caught in a conundrum in that Dave didn't want us to go on without them, and he didn't desire for him and Shelly to climb out without us. It proved a paradox. An 8:00 am departure went a long way toward proving intent on their part. We busted ass and traveled 5 miles, half of the remaining distance to the Rio Loera confluence. We made the Arroyo Ahuichique after covering 8 to 9 miles. The immense geology here is punctuated with cacti, palms, and all manner of trees and spiny things. The walls of the canyon rose hundreds of feet. The coloration would put an artist's pallet to shame. Pushing hard tomorrow, like today, would yield camping just shy of Guerachi. That way, we would be poised to enter Guerachi at midmorning. I encountered a Tarahumara man who seemed to dash out to confront me. When I asked him if he spoke Spanish he replied, "No sabe." I imagine he wanted us to hit the highway.

"Being in a Canyon this immense gives the feel of caving. You are in a trap of your own making. A glorious trap. Light, water, life—very uncave like, but still. Dave harvested big time today. He probably is drying about ¼ lb. at least. It budded, tasty, & good. He is a maniac. The Taras. don't give a Rat's Ass about us being here. They are not friendly and they are not engaging. HIWAY! Maybe Guerachi is enough Mexican so as to be cool."

The Arroyo Pittorreal was passed as we approached the Rio Loera, where we set up camp at the confluence. A large pool fronted our beach property, located in such a beautiful place as to defy adjectives, and a swim was forced in order to have a look-see up the spectacular Rio Loera. It was flowing with equal volume, as were both the Rio Turuachi and Arroyo Guachochi. The Rio Verde was now truly righteous on this **Friday, the 13th**.

"Scott and I dropped off our packs and made the swim to have a look-see up the Lorea. It is fantastic, with about equal water as the Rio Turuachi had. We are all exhausted. Today was a true Canyoneering day. We dropped the distance between 100m. marks through probably the toughest reach yet faced. Very exhausting, big boulders, lots of swims, and plenty of just plain ass-kicking pack carrying. After this stretch, the Meter marks spread way out for the duration. This hopefully will equate to easier going, at least to Guerachi where some or all must contemplate exiting!"

With the spreading out of the 100-meter contour lines, we had predicted that the topography left to encounter should equate to easier going from here on out, and sure enough, **Saturday** proved a rather featureless day. The distance left between us and Guerachi should be equal to a long canyon day's walk, some nine to 10 crow-fly miles. What hadn't been predicted was running into the Mexican Army.

After leaving the Rio Loera confluence, I topped out on a riverbank rise and spotted a rifle-toting, camouflage-wearing, obvious Mexican soldier. My immediate inclination was to just keep walking. As Tom was right behind me, we came along together. We came alongside the soldier and we exchanged pleasantries. I looked upon the hill to my left, and I could see there were many soldiers. I could also see an awning-covered command post and soldiers with binoculars. Tom and I decided to await the others, and shortly they came along, escorted at gunpoint. Dave and Shelly had entered the water to the amusement of the soldiers, and I prepared for trouble. The soldier I had first encountered received a radio transmission with an order to just let us go on our way. Dave and Shelly stopped moving in the water to inquire as to what was going to happen. As Dave stood up, revealing his six-foot four-inch frame, a streak of marijuana shake was clearly visible across the front of his wetsuit. He apparently had entered the water to dump his stash after retrieving it from his camera pouch. He could then distractingly snap photos of the soldiers while flinging his plastic pot bag's contents. In the process, he managed to paint a racer stripe of Mota that accentuated his wet garb. I silently motioned for him to look down. Noticing the stripe, he slipped back into the water to wash it off. I am fairly certain the soldiers were too in awe of Dave's stature and pretty Shelly to notice the faux pas. I decided to immediately cross the river, and the others followed. I wanted to distance the Army. Once in the water and following a few crossing, I rid myself of my pocketed smoke. While I had been tempted to not dump my stash, I thought it best to step away from the table. While swimming a box, I encountered a small tied-off plastic bag of the Sensi, and I snagged it as I recognized it was Dean's. Again, while swimming another box, I came upon the same plastic bag. This time, in my zeal to retrieve it, I neglected to exit the box in time to avoid a gnarly bit of rapid running as the box came to an end. At least that evening, we had herb.

"The wind kicked up last nite & filled my hair and bag with sand. It was a pleasant evening, however. Cont. I'm fantasizing about the possible climb out at Guerachi. According to a Soldier I asked, there is no Pueblo there, no food."

I really did not like the Army's unsolicited intrusion into my canyon mind. The Army incident really didn't sit well with me. Upon reaching Guerachi we would all most likely exit. The contour lines indicated that the canyoneering portion of this canyon had already been accomplished. With the interpersonal relating being what they had become, and having seen the canyoneering stretch of this canyon, what we would be missing if we were to climb out at Guerachi was the village of Batopilas. As I had been there already, I didn't feel like I would be missing out. Scott is bummed if we were to not make Batopilas. Dean spoke of going it solo if need be.

"Cont. We are riding out the hot part of the day before entering Guerachi. The plan is to climb a couple of mi. out this afternoon, camp, and then finish the climb tomorrow. This sits well with everyone. Except possibly Dean who may go it solo (?). Scott has been sick the last two days w/o telling anyone. I suspected as much by his energy level of late. He is so strong & stoic! Tom and Dean have dropped (LSD) a half each. I have no interest in that at all. Too much on my mind. I miss Gail, and I'm now eager for the exit. Cont. El Llano Salado is apparently abandoned. It is full of Prickly Poppies— an indication of overgrazing. Old stone structures & walls (roll #9 B.&W.!) stand in mute testimony to past history. #'s cans of poison (Herbicide?) lay strewn about. Some cattle, Feral Pigs, and two shade-loving Burros are the only inhabitants we have seen. This may possibly have been the Bread Basket for the Town of Guerachi at one time. In its' silence, it is very sad."

I had a **Sunday** stroll around El Llano Salado looking for errant Dean and Tom. I followed a tunnel-like path into the mesquite trees and came upon an enormous bull lounging while passing away the heat of the day in a shady hidey-hole. I gingerly made my way far from the bull, back into the clearing. I heard crashing, and Dean emerged with a big grin on his face. Half the day was spent at our El Lano Salado camp while Dean and Tom sought doors of perception in the mesquite trees.

We made Guerachi at 4:00 in the afternoon after encountering some serious bouldering down canyon 1.5 miles before reaching it. It was an amazing encore presented to us by the canyon. Dean said it was spooky. On entering Guerachi, I immediately met Aldegundo and Benito Loera, father and son. I addressed the elder Aldegundo, and he turned to his son to ask him if he understood me. Benito responded, "Si," and we were all set to communicate. Guerachi is a former village, just a collection of houses now. There would be no tienda here. Benito told us to follow them.

We were introduced to Javier Lopez, a young man who manned the CFE Station (Commission Federal Electricidad, a river-gauging station). There were huge citrus trees, peaches, apples, chickens, pigs, cows, goats, and gardens. It was like a paradise lost. We were taken to the Loera home, where we met the wife of Aldegundo, Petronilla Loera. Benito and I became fast friends. They allowed us to camp on their property, giving us all the fruit we could eat. Javier allowed us to use his kitchen to cook dinner. That evening, as they had learned that I was a medic, Benito's was sent over with a bombed-out molar toothache. A Q-Tip cleaning with oil of clove and a Percocet supplemented with Tylenol had him rendered one happy camper. I advised the Loera family that Benito should still see a dentist to get that tooth pulled. I left them with some more Tylenol.

Monday morning had Benito experiencing a miracle cure, and Aldegundo was very pleased. We contracted with them to arrange a ride to Guachochi from the trail's end. Javier had radio contact at his gauging station that could facilitate this. After our long and steep climb out, with Benito requesting to hike with us, there would be a ride waiting to take us into Guachochi.

"Lunch with the Loera Family was a pleasant surprise. Cafe Negro con asuca, Hard-Boiled Eggs (Rosa colored!) and Bean Burritos with Atun y Picante. It was excellent. I suspect that Aldegundo hiked out to arrange the ride and to have himself and Petronilla meet us at the ⅔ point, by a little stream with lunch all ready to eat at 12:00 noon."

The "guide" service, lunch, and the ride cost us a grand total of $50.00. I am always happy to have a positive economic impact down in Mexico, like with Federico at the beginning of our trip. The Loera family has an extensive history and relationship with life in the Barranca Sinforosa. The namesake Rio Loera enters just a few miles up the river. They report no knowledge of any people before us having traveled down this Barranca as we did. I told them that they might begin seeing more "travelers" like us. They also told us that the Mexican Army was back in the canyon to follow up on their previous drug eradication efforts. Apparently, it was them responsible for the chopped-up water tubing and the empty cans of herbicide. We had a truck ride to Guachochi waiting for us at the trailhead.

A stay in Guachochi was very appreciated as several group members felt ill. I went in search of my colitis medication with no luck. We moved to the city of Hidalgo del Parral, the location of the assassination of Pancho Villa. There I had no greater luck with finding my medicine. A night spent drinking at the "New York" bar had us running into a group of drunk and rowdy Mexican drug dealers. Their leader prevented me from exiting the restroom by throwing his legs across my path. He insisted we speak English and went on to tell me that if we were there to do business, we would do business with him. I told him I would certainly keep that in mind. Tom left back to the U.S. of his own volition, but getting shy of Dave and Shelly was proving difficult as they didn't want to take any initiative separate from the group. I was just feeling exhausted in body and soul, homesick, and now very sick with colitis.

"Fri. 3/20/92

I'm sitting here at the Chamizal National Memorial sans the rest of the group. They are all still downtown at or near the Bus Station, I presume. It became too much to hang out with them anymore. We left Parral after 9:00 last night and, after an uneventful and restless night, arrived in Juarez about 4:30 am. At 6:00, we were able to board a bus bound for the El Paso Bus Station. The cost of $14,000 Pesos, and the entry into the U.S. was rather painless. Dean admitted to having Fruit, and he was the only one subjected to a pack check. There was a nice old Mexican Gentleman who sat next to Dean and *told wonderful stories of a life spent as a Mining Engineer in Mexico. He talked of Batopilas—the History, the Poppies, his travels there by plane before the road existed. I asked him if Chamizal was within walking distance of the International Bridge we had just crossed. Due to his mistaking our x-ing location, he said no. It turns out we were right next to it and could see it from the Bus as we entered the Freeway. At this point, Dave groaned and proceeded to freak, asking if I could get the Driver to stop the Bus. I said, "Why don't you try." I was fed up with this look of despair and of carrying him & Shell. When we got to the Greyhound Station, I asked the Driver if he would pass by the National Monument again—he gave me the old "Why didn't you get off there in the 1st place" line, with great disgust with us looks. I just lost it. Everyone was inquiring about what had transpired, and I just wanted out of there. Women started asking me to retrieve their luggage from underneath the bus while Scott stood mutely by. I had to leave and quickly. I grabbed my stuff and retreated to a nearby Jack-In-The-Box for breakfast and solitude. The weirdos were out in full force. Some Buck-Wheat looking motherfucker, A grinning psycho type. A grinning middle age faggot. I had to shit so bad, I left my backpack and waited, bowels screaming while some asshole made leisure noises from the one crapper the restroom had. Madly I dashed back to my pack to find the grinning faggot waiting. I went out the door to the expediency of a Taxi and Chamizal. My bowels had subsided, and I could have a Human exchange with the Driver. He dropped me off, and immediately, the tremendous urge to defecate hit, frantically I tried the Monument (locked!), looked for Porta-Potties (none), and was proceeding to shit my pants when I let loose in the relative privacy of a small space by a side door. My hand and plenty of dirt serving as T.P.! Now I wait inside the Visitor Center for someone to talk with about all of us being here. They opened the doors promptly at 8:00 am, but no one is at the front desk. It is a big Visitor Center inside with a very big Green Lawn compound right next to the River. I talked with the Ranger, and he said it was OK if we hung out and waited. I'm not expecting the others very soon, which is just as well. I behaved badly, and I'm enjoying this time to myself. Being here at Chamizal is a fitting end to this sojourn. The Mexican and the American flag flap overhead. There is a steady stream of traffic crossing the bridge from Mexico. This place has a real Park feel to it, which I guess is the intent. People jog the outer perimeter, and some stroll the grounds. Sitting here, I feel the fool for losing my cool the way I did. I truly hate when that happens. Strange, strange trip. Soon I will go, call the Hilton in L.C. to connect with my love. Gail is truly special and very patient with me. She is not too excited about S&D. This is in keeping with my having to carry them. They feigned absolute helplessness almost the whole trip. Shell is so much more capable than that. I believe that Dave drags down her confidence to match his own fears. He never seemed to actually be on our expedition. His mind was always somewhere else. His constant chatter was slowly driving us all to madness. Although very strong, he wasn't up for such a great endeavor! I believe Shell performed well, and I'm afraid it wasn't enough. Dean and I speak of possibly the Barranca Guaynopa without any extraneous personalities, i.e. Dean, Scott, and I. I fear even Gail is not up to Canyoneering on this scale. We can push ourselves to the limits of dying but cannot expect this from others. Dean and Scott are very strong. Possibly more so than I, and seem connected with the idea of these big, possibly 1st descents."*

Dean, Scott, Russell – Urique, 1991

Naphi, Jody, Susan, Russell – Barranca Del Cobre, 1987

Baku, Mars, Jody, Susan – Barranca Del Cobre, 1987 (RJR)

Jane, Scott, Gail, Dean, Russell – Barranca Del Cobre, 1991

Bryan Thomas – Barranca Batopilas, 1993 (RJR)

Dean and Jane – Barranca Batopilas, 1993 (RJR)

Dean Bruemmer – Barranca Del Cobre, 1991 (RJR)

Dean, Russell, Scott – Barranca Urique Dump, 1991

Dr. Gail Willow – Barranca Del Cobre, 1991 (RJR)

Barranca Sinforosa Rock Calving, 1992 (RJR)

James and Marie Ray – Mexico, 2002 (RJR)

Jane – Barranca Sinforosa, 1993 (RJR)

Jane – Barranca Del Cobre, 1991 (RJR)

Barranca Sinforosa, 1992 (RJR)

Russell – Cascada Recubirachi, 1994 (Alice Cohen)

Russell – Gran Salto, 1993 (Dean Bruemmer)

Russell – Vertical Vietnam, 1993 (Dean Bruemmer)

Russell – Barranca Sinforosa, 1992 (Dean Bruemmer)

Scott Steinberg – Barranca Sinforosa, 1992 (RJR)

Russell – Piedras Del Lumbre, 2001 (Martha Anderson)

Russell and Sonia – Apache Warm Springs, 2003

Barranca Del Cobre, 1991 (RJR)

Barranca Del Cobre, 1991 (RJR)

Vertical Vietnam Gorge, 1994 (Dean Bruemmer)

Chapter 5
Barranca Batopilas:
Part 1, 1993

Friday, the 5th of February, 1993, had us boarding a bus bound for Parral. Jody and Rex were back for shuttle duty to the border between El Paso and Juarez. Once dropped off, we shouldered our packs and walked over the San Francisco bridge only to find "La Miga" was closed. We hiked a couple of blocks over to the 24-hour crossing station. From there, we were able to breeze through into Mexico armed with visas. It took two taxis to get all five of us canyoneers and our gear to the Juarez Bus Station.

"Jody left me with, "I hope you come back with your head screwed on straight." This had special meaning to her, I suppose! Our relationship is strained to say the least. It is our nature to clash at this time. We are five strong and determined people with expectations for this endeavor."

Thank the gods for Dean and Scott. They were my anchors that I truly knew were up for all of this. Jane, from both the 1990 and 1991 Barranca del Cobre trips, was back. She would hopefully have a grounding effect on my potential antic-driven behaviors. She was nursing a recent knee injury and harboring fears of the cold water. Bryan was a roommate friend of ours who had recently thrown in with sharing a "Batch Pad" along with Dean, Tom, Steve, and me.

Gail and I had divorced shortly after my return from last year's Sinforosa expedition after 16 years of marriage, which included her becoming a dentist. She finally admitted to not wanting children after all the years of us holding off. I had begun to feel lost in life as I had such a strong desire to be a father, and fighting fires while being married to a dentist had me feeling a major disconnect in my life. Gail and I still loved each other, but sadly, it was just time to go our separate ways.

I had gotten involved with the film industry as well as with a practicing Wican, while living in the small mountain town of Kingston, New Mexico. I drank way too much, and I had maniacal energy. Both helped me with running away from myself. Lindy was not a good little Witch. She tended toward the dark side of life. She manifested a horror my puny scientific education could not ascribe to any Periodic Table. We put in a massive effort to visit all the out-of-the-way bars in southern New Mexico and Arizona, where plenty of mischiefs was to be found. A pseudo knife fight and rancher ménage à trois were par for the course of my strange spiraling life. Christmas Eve 1992 had me having a drunken argument with the bar patrons in Cuchillo, New Mexico. I was too inebriated to believe them telling me it was the day before Christmas, as I was scheduled to cook Christmas dinner for a Black Range Lodge full of people back in Kingston. Lindy and I beat a hasty retreat.

With this canyon expedition, the plan was to document it with both still pictures and video. This added a different component that we would attempt our best to take seriously, and as the financing was all on me, I felt a certain pressure to come through with worthwhile footage. In Guachochi, we secured a truck ride along a dirt road that terminated at Gran Salto (Cascada Recubirachi). It is a spectacular 20+meter fall where the road ends. The road actually ends a ways back upriver, and the need was to continue driving in the Rio Batopilas to end up parked at the falls.

"Mon. 2/8/93

Cont. 6:00 pm We have just finished Dinner (Potatoes, & Gravy ala Bryan!) and are situated above a massive (100 ft.!) fall on the Rio Batopilas. This place is awesome, and according to the map, it represents the end of the road, just beyond Saterachi. It begins to cloud up after what was a gorgeous, warm, mostly sunny day. I'm sort of mad at Jane because of equipment stuff, but I will get over it! She tries."

"Tues. 2/9/93

We are at camp #1, the spot above the Falls (Gran Salto / Cascada Recubirachi) on the Rio Batopilas. It pretty much rained all last night and continues to sprinkle this morning. It is hard to think about breaking camp and get going. The guys are trying to start a fire. Jane sorts through her stuff in our tent while I write. Last night's rain caused problems with all except Bryan, Jane, & me. We will perfect this. Funny, it seems we should have already perfected it by now. I hope for a break in the weather. I will hike in my Wetsuit since I can't afford to get my Camp clothes wet. This should be interesting. The color coordination and all!"

The first day in the Canyon had us traveling five miles downriver to reach camp no. 2. The terrain was not too rough, and no swimming was required. The rain and drizzle, along with heavy packs, made it hard to get into the groove. I dumped three times on slick rocks and ended seated to my waist in the very cold water. Camp 2 was in a cave approximately 30 feet above a placid Rio Batopilas. A roaring fire soon had us all feeling toasty. Large boulders were beginning to appear in the river bottom. The canyon is very spectacular and temperate at this point and populated with a lot of conifers.

I was experiencing a delayed getting-into-this syndrome. I missed Gail, but I also missed Lindy the Witch. I didn't know what to do with my life beyond attempting a potential first descent of this unknown Barranca Batopilas. I wanted this as some kind of potential catharsis to verge off a path of potential madness and self-destruction. The mood was proving somber, made more so I believe by the video project. My back was killing me as my old injury was just getting older. It started raining hard as soon as the cave was moved into. I maintained it was because of my psychic abilities. Dean said, "Bullshit!" I then admitted it was my gammy knee acting as a barometer. Dean was leery of my delving into a Wican World. I am sure his concerns were heartfelt. An old Tarahumara gentleman had inquired as to our destination. He was amazed and stated his belief that no one had done that before and that we were better off climbing into the Sierra instead.

On **Wednesday**, we made it to just shy of where the map shows the trail on the canyon bottom (that we hadn't been following) exiting. We had taken the map trail marking to indicate that passage along the river was possible through this stretch we had been breezing through. While it was fairly evident that the topographical information on the map indicated easy terrain, this was in comparison to what the topo maps indicated would be encountered further down the canyon. From the "trail" endpoint shown on the map, there are no more inhabitants indicated along the river. There was a bridge across the river where the map indicated a vado. This was apparently the end of the civilized world. A Tarahumara fisherman had come along, and with one cast of his hand-held line, he pulled out a fish. A Mexican Rancher rode up on horseback accompanied by a teenage Tarahumara girl on foot, as well as a shivering dog. The girl kept nervously slapping her thigh with a large hunting knife as I spoke with the rancher. He was rather amused with our asses and wondered why we weren't using the trail. We were speaking together right on the river, so apparently, there was a trail leading to this vado that he had been following. We had not bothered to look for it.

"Dinner was courtesy of Dean. An excellent noodle dish complete with Ramen Noodles that toured the Sinforosa and dried Squash from the Hardware Store in Parral, bought last year. It really was excellent. I ate a lot. This trip is really hard to figure. The whole feel is so unique to this trip. I don't believe it is because of the Video project either. It is truly amazing here. We are starting to come out of the Conifer Zone. They are far fewer, scragalier, and not as large through this stretch. The sky is partly cloudy, and the night promises to be rainless (?)! I climbed a large boulder in Camp to finish writing this entry. It

is so amazing here!"

Last night was super chilly, with a layer of frost over everything. My wet river shoes were frozen solid, and I had to piss on them, so I could get them thawed enough to put them on. As we were faced with a probability of needing to swim today, we were glad that this Thursday had dawned clear. We are covering 7 to 8 kilometers a day map distance, so we were on schedule. Jane is OK with her knee, but she confesses worries to me about what lies ahead. I didn't know how to allay her fears beyond the usual cliched platitudes like, "It will be alright." Though the day was strenuous, there were no swims. It is definitely a barranca here. It is very boulder-choked and the water is the familiarly beautiful emerald green color. Agua cristal is indicative of manageable water flow. Agua Negra indicates flooding. Floating logs mean the river is still rising. The canyon was dropping rapidly through this gorgeous stretch. The water volume was not yet extreme, and thusly the crossings were not too difficult. Our camp was struck on a vegetated ledge 40 feet above the river. That afforded a precaution against high water flooding.

"Fri. 2/12/93 5:14 pm

Today's progress amounted to only a couple of miles. This is for several reasons, the main of which is the failure of the hard diving cases to keep the Cameras dry. Disaster!!!! One Camera down (the large one!) and adios for the DAT. I have a feeling the Camera will rise from the Ashes, but that feeling is not so strong for the DAT! Such is life. By the time this was discovered, we had made a couple of very cold swims on a cloudy day in this narrow part of the Canyon. We stopped to make a warming fire, and here we stayed. This worked for the best since I may have cracked a rib(s) when I took a spectacular splat on my face. It hurts pretty well now! After the rib fall, we had to negotiate a ledge drop into a swim. I lowered my pack after having thrown my stick. Just as I was releasing the pack, I noticed the stick motoring up, under the ledge, followed closely by my pack. I hurriedly took a plunge into what I should have down climbed into, not worrying about ankle impact on the cobbly bottom nor the clearance of my backside from the ledge. Wham, I took a hard punch in the left Kidney from the ledge. I was too self-absorbed in saving my Gear and myself from a nasty trip through a cobweb-filled, half submerged, dark, cold corridor to notice Dean hollering, 'Be more careful Russell!'"

As Dean was a smoker, I asked him for a drag off his cigarette, and he said, "Be careful Russell, that's how it starts." Not being a cigarette smoker had me catch quite the nicotine buzz. I needed to calm the fuck down after the equipment failure. Financial pragmatics didn't need a seat at this table where they didn't belong.

"Cont. This, our 5th Camp is situated in a most spectacular part of the Canyon. The Rio really drops through here, and the Canyon bottom is narrow (100ft.), and very boulder choked. This intensity is guaranteed for at least a few more days, possibly a week. It will kick our asses. We will emerge changed, I feel. How can we not? Each in our own way knows the intensity

& meaning of this trip. Jane says it is the Old Foggie trip. I fear she is right. I'm not the person of six years ago who first descended when I was 10,000 days old. My prime, it seems. I got such a late start on all of this. I fear it is all becoming a finished Chapter of my life! I feel the need to write a lot. As I should since I aspire to be some kind of writer someday! This trip is another in a long line of experience gathering events for my great quest to make a living with words. And the visual, film & video! I think I have Director's vision. I'm a director, that is for sure. Is my life heading this way, kind of like the Rio we descend? Or is the Rio ascending? Gravity does play such tricks! My trouble with focusing is pronounced still, yet I know what I want. To live beyond these Canyon Walls and to inhabit my home, and there, fall in Love with myself. I so desperately need this. This is about myself. When whole again (if ever!), then maybe I can be seen. Can be fit for Human company!"

We were definitely in the meat and potatoes of this canyon. The drop was so intense, and it was nonstop Boulder Field City. With only some swimming made warmer by mostly walking, bouldering, and crashing through vegetation along forested steep side slopes. It is like a saving grace to have these slopes as it was conceivable to have had only vertical walls. Walls with boulders between them. From certain aspects, it was like a hallway filled with giant rocks and a canyon bottom so narrow as to defy belief. At one point, we had to lower the packs by rope so we could safely downclimb. Past Arroyo Aboreachi, the only extreme effort was seeing us through. It was true wilderness. What a way to spend a **Saturday**.

"I am camped separately from the main group. This is for several reasons. #1 of which is that I like my Beach spot! Enough said, short of I'm still losing my mind. Too bad! It is a bowl:30 in the Canyon. Bryan is baking some kind of Jalapeno Pie for Dinner. The way to Batopilas is not straight & narrow, only narrow and boulder choked! At least navigation is no problem since only one direction can be taken. The only real analogy I can come to is Caving. We are Spelunking this situation. This is so awesome!"

Yesterday while scrounging for firewood, Dean found a wooden Tarahumara kickball. He also found "Bob," a carved wooden totem that was aptly named for its obvious mode of transportation. Dean will now carry the waterlogged artifact, which we estimated weighed five pounds. Upon drying it should lose weight. Bob was a Celestial Hitchhiker on the Batopilas Highway. Dean is the Indiana Jones of the canyons. We have affected a measured pace. We mostly push, with two 15-minute and one ½-hour breaks for videoing, photos, rest, snacks, water, sunscreen, and buzzing. **Sunday** had not been a day of rest as the need to keep moving was an always prescient feeling.

"Cont. 4:45 pm

Camp is at a little Overhang with a Beach fronting it. This place was the issue of some debate. It is large enough to accommodate the two w/o tents. Jane and I share a tent. Bryan has his own. What happened was that after hiking all day in the Rain, as well as swimming, we were pretty much tapped. This was after a two-warming fire day! Anyhow, at this overhang,

Scott & Dean went to scout a better "Cave," crucial, since there is a lack of portable shelter. B., J., & I stayed to start a warming fire, and the rest is history. D & S had actually scouted a quote, 'big Cave, with lots of dry wood,' but it was too late. We of the warming fire were already situated. Dean is bummed! Cont. 6:26 pm, time to start hunkering down for the evening. Dinner was excellent, care of Jane. I cannot begin to describe how hard today's going was. Right out of Camp, it was intense. Add the almost constant drizzle and rain it was very interesting, tiring, bone-jarring, and all in all, one hell of a day. We only covered approx. 3.5 linear miles today. This is, of course, five+ as we go miles! If the weather will only break, we can make much further pushes. The cold is what eats my lunch. I start losing coordination, concentration, and just plain willpower. I fantasize about my warm, electric blanket-powered cama and fiery lover Lindy! I do miss her! Coffee, late in bed, warm soaks with Grolsh Beers and goofing. Here is to you, my Lover. Salud!!! We are all very tired. Tired acting & tired looking."

Monday had me making no journal entries. We had holed up in a large cave complete with a spring that appeared to serve as a Tarahumara goat pen. It was poised a couple of hundred feet above the Rio Batopilas, which had risen dramatically in an accumulative effect from all the precipitation we had been receiving. The Agua Negra was enough to be of concern to us with regards to continuing through this very steep canyon stretch we found ourselves in. The decision had been made to scout along the very steep side slope for a safer way around a tricky narrow high-water flow section. We had reached a meander that had a backside that appeared truly undoable, with tight walls and big boulders. Bryan found the cave, and we decided to bag it for the day. It was too steep to find a vantage that afforded a clear view into a river that appeared to be rife with all kinds of hydraulic river nasties. This was proving to be a potential endpoint as the group wanted to call it quits. Bryan said it was like a "Vertical Vietnam" and that you needed to rope up to take a shit.

I scouted for a rappel point to get past the box of death, and I found a bamboo-covered ledge with a drop of about 75 feet to the rushing water below. As that water poured into a very large box pool, I felt it was a place we could regain the river again after a rappel. We could then meet up with our packs that we would have heaved into the river preceding our rappel. I returned to the cave camp to report my finding to the unconvinced crew. Bryan, who had been a very steady team member, stated, "I didn't know you were willing to die for this." I told him to stop being so dramatic. I grabbed the rope bag and proceeded to retrace my downclimb to the bamboo-covered ledge. It was so sketchy that I needed to throw the rope bag to free up both my hands. When I threw the bag, it caught a hefty branch. The branch served as a catapult and away went the bag arching through the air on its way over the precipice. I exclaimed, "Fuck" as it was game over without the rope. I downclimbed more for the last look-see, and there was the rope bag snagged on a bush. I proceeded to clear the ledge of bamboo with a Swiss Army Knife saw.

That accomplished, I climbed back to the cave to report the progress on the plan. This was met with silence. Dean said he wanted to check it out himself. We downclimbed to the now-cleared ledge. We laid down side by side to peer over the edge at the rushing water below. Dean shook his head, and as it was so loud with the sound of the roaring water, he had to yell that Jane and Bryan wouldn't even come down to contemplate the feasibility. It was game over. Back at the cave, I admonished the group along the lines of "when the going gets tough." Dean told me he didn't trust my leadership anymore, nor my state of mind. I shot back with my not believing he ever did. I said I would go on solo, and Dean said they would have to drug and hogtie me to get me out. Talk about someone being dramatic. I was actually just despondent and feeling defeated. What an anticlimax to this dream of a cathartic first descent. I silently acquiesced to an exit strategy.

"Weds. 2/17/93

We are situated approx. 10 mi. from our Cave Camp and definitely out of the Canyon! This camp is approx. ⅔ the distance to the road to Guachochi & Creel. Also, we will connect with the road to Batopilas and thus have the possibility of actually going to Batopilas for a short stay. Only tomorrow will tell just what will happen! After yesterday's "Vertical Vietnam," complete with the rappel staging area and a launch zone hacked with a Swiss Army knife saw into the dense Bamboo stand covering the overhanging ledge from which we proposed to rappel to the waiting River, we are all ready for a break, Cerveza, a hot shower (or 2 or 3!) and a very comfortable bed. Round this off with a home-cooked meal (Red Chicken Enchiladas!), and we should be right for more adventuring, whatever that may be.

I guess for me, the fact is that I'm not in a hurry to go home, since I really don't have a home as such to be in a hurry to go home to! I wish it were so. I do miss my former life. I'm still in Love with Gail! This presents problems."

"Thurs. 2/18/93 approx. 2:30

We sit in a restaurant in Aboreachi. Dead tired and dirty as hell. We covered approx. 12 or 13 for today, that with the 10+ mi. of yesterday makes upwards of 25 mi. to get out of the Barranca Batopilas back to civilization. There are buses to Creel & Guachochi, twice a day! Creel is reportedly three ½ hrs. & Guachochi 1 hr. This would make the time from Creel to Guachochi four ½ hrs. I don't believe this to be true. W/o the maps, it is impossible to tell anything. The maps I speak of being San Juanito & Samachique, which I left in Kingston, rolled up with a signed "Paper Hearts" poster. Remnants of Sundance! It is decision central in Aboreachi. Should we stay or should we go? We can rent Cabanas and stay the night, or we could try to rent a ride to Creel via Truck. I would love to make Creel tonight. This would mean a hot shower for sure. The Cabanas apparently have water, but I doubt it is hot water for showering. We shall see! 25 mi. out. Fantastic! One report of the distance back to the road was 30+ Kilometers. This was not believed at the time, but guess what, the distance was greater. We smelled Beer, so we did what should have taken three days, we did in two!!! Time to think of getting going. We can check on the ride, Bus, Cabana situation and then make decisions based on the reality of what is possible!

Gail. Gail, Gail, Gail, everywhere I turn, Gail! Still such an impact on my life. My strange life. I fear I'm losing my entire past, along with my voice. It is as if I will be all alone, without my friends who are dear to me. I'm a stranger to them, I'm strange to them. Dean believes my mind to have gone off. We argued in the Canyon. He told me that he no longer trusted my judgment, my leadership. Bitter words they were for me. They hurt a lot, especially coming from Dean. He is a great, good friend, but I'm losing that along with other aspects of my life. This trip is so strange & wondrous on many different levels. I look across the Railroad Tracks at my Friends."

It took us two days to hike back to Aboreachi from the Cave Camp. Along the way, we passed a ranchito where an immunization clinic for the Tarahumaras was being conducted. We heard the Tarahumara drums announcing the event long before we got to the clinic location, just like we had heard them on several occasions announcing our presence down in the canyons. The doctor and the nurses were very pleased with seeing us, and they spoke about how tourist dollars would prove very helpful to the rampant poverty the Tarahumara existed under. It is my understanding that the Tarahumara Tribe is second in size only to the Navajo Nation and that they had always occupied the best fertile land until the arrival of the Spaniards had forced them into the safety of the Barrancas. It is a harsh life dependent on the rains and famine is a constant threat.

Upon reflection, I felt terrible about my canyon departure reaction. Dean is one of my best friends ever. We were roommates. We have been on so many adventures, as well as several Search and Rescue missions together. I trust him with my life. My blind singlemindedness had me behaving quite badly. Some months after the expedition, while at a party, Dean and Scott told me they had been scared. I was really taken aback; as the last thing I would have suspected had occurred was for my brave friends to have experienced fear. The attempts to be filmmakers had added a component that not only cost me a bundle, it also took energy away from the real task at hand. Multitasking is supposedly being scientifically proven to be a fallacy. Perhaps so, but what is certain is that a person can only really wear one hat at a time. Was I a canyoneer, a filmmaker, or was I just somebody getting lost in the canyons of his mind?

Looking back, I am truly amazed at what we had accomplished, especially in light of the fact that we had to deal with days of precipitation. That alone was manageable, but what wouldn't have been possible to deal with was a flash flood. The Barranca Batopilas is a mile deep. A canyon that is a mile deep makes for one hell of a watershed. Such a large watershed could generate a flash flood of Biblical proportions. In hindsight, we really had providence on our side. We just charged ahead armed with the knowledge that nature is not benign.

After bailing on the canyon descent attempt Bryan and I made our way into Batopilas. From there, he hiked up and over to the village of Urique while I made my way around to meet up with him in five days' time. I came upon him in the Urique Village Plaza sitting with a new friend, Micah True. Micah was over from Batopilas, where he lived. He went by the handle of "Caballo Blanco." He told me he was a long-distance runner who ran with the Tarahumara. They are famous for their long-distance running. Micah would go on to be a world-famous runner, thanks to the book "Born to Run" (Christopher McDougall, 2009). From Urique, Bryan and I made our way back to Creel so Bryan could meet with a girl from Silver City. Margarita gave me a room in her new hotel as she figured I was good for business. The three girls we knew from Silver City, New Mexico, invited themselves to stay in my room as I had drunkenly agreed to guide them to the canyon bottom the next day. The next day I accompanied them to the canyon rim and told them to pay strict attention to my instructions. I then bid them adieu.

From Creel, we made our way to Los Mochis by train in order to film the mouth of the Rio Verde located by the fishing village of El Colorado. This adventure included a lively drunken incident of scaling the train locomotive and getting thrown into our seats, with Bryan exclaiming, "Now they won't sell us beer." The Mesero immediately showed up with a bucket of ice-cold beer. The people of El Colorado took us under their wing. We stayed with our new friend Taclchito and his family. We played pickup basketball. They cranked up the outdoor theatre to show an American movie. We took a high-speed Ponga ride through the mangrove forest and went right on out into the Pacific Ocean via the mouth of the Rio Fuerte. The fishermen all liked to smoke really tasty Sensimilla.

After leaving El Colorado, we were able to board the 11-hour ferry ride to La Paz at Topolobampo. Bryan got seasick as a dog after I warned him not to eat the chicken enchiladas on offer in the ship galley. We had fun in the sun for a week of pseudo debauchery spent hanging out with the Canadian pirate David. Bryan almost drowned in the powerful Pacific surf on a beach where two German tourists had died the week before (San Pedrito). There is a wicked rip current in place. After dragging his ass into his sleeping bag, I went to stay at the Hotel California with a German girl in Todos Santos, where we danced the night away. I had met Heidelinde in Divisadero, and as she was a woman of means, she flew over to meet up with us in Baja Sur. We got to see the "Mexican Madonna" at the Palenque after playing beach soccer with her band and getting an exclusive invite. The drunken revelry was followed by Bryan staggering into a minefield of human waste outside the arena and then getting all comfy in his sleeping bag. The next day, I insisted he trash the shitty bag in lieu of putting it in the rental car.

It was time to go home, wherever that was. I was tired from running. Tired of traversing the canyons of my mind.

Chapter 6
Barranca Batopilas:
Part 2, 1994

"Sat. 1/29/94

We crossed the border at 11:30 after obtaining Insurance in Deming. -$280.00 for 31 days, yuk! The border experience was really easy as well as the Federal Police stop near Janos. He asked a few times about Guns, "Not even just one Machine Gun." It was 10:30 pm (NM) time by the time we made Creel and the Hotel Koreachi. It was cold, late, I was tired, and Dean was sick, so we got one room for all of us. Scott and I sit in Margarita's, eating breakfast before the drive to Aboreachi and the start of our hike! Margarita is upset that we didn't stay with her, and she says that we can't eat here and not expect to stay here! She is a sweet shark. She well remembers Bryan and me from last year. The drive to Aboreachi should take 3+ hrs. Today dawned clear & cold. I hope the weather holds! I do believe that we are becoming connected now. Jane and Dean have shown up, and Margarita continues her harangue! Cont. 12:25 pm. We are in Aboreachi now, back at the "no-name" Restaurant where we ate last year. I hope to find a place to park the car for the walk into the Rio Batopilas! The food is so good here. Simple and good! We can park the car for the trip duration at Dilia Acosta's for $25.00! This is payable to Carlos Acosta. Cont. 4:30 pm We are now situated back at old camp

#10 and definitely on the trail in. This Camp is approx. 10 mi in. Carlos, the Son of Dilia, consented to let us park our vehicle at the restaurant and to giving us a ride to approx. seven mi in along the rough road to a point just shy of Aboreachi. We then walked approx. two ½ mi more to reach our old Camp of last year. The Creek is dry, as are all the Drainages, including the Urique & Batopilas? I hope so, but water may be a problem tomorrow!"

We were back to try to complete what had been denied to us last year. This year we would make it to the bridge at La Bufa. For this attempt, there were four of us: Dean, Scott, Jane, and myself. We had a resolve that didn't include a need to be videographers. While we would do videotaping along the way, we would just be canyoneers. The fact that it appeared to be drier than last year sat well with us as the river was most likely down. I woke up the first Sunday spent on the way back into the canyon with both the inside and outside of my bivy sack coated with frost. The moon had been full, and the night was punctuated with the rhythm of a fitful cold night's sleep. We were very hopeful of making the Cave Camp of last year by day's end. Five days of canyoneering from there should put us at the La Bufa bridge. From there, we could return to Aboreachi to retrieve my vehicle.

"We made it back to the Cave camp after leaving camp at 9:00 am and hiking till 4:00 pm. We are all very tired."

I cooked dinner that evening. Cajun rice for hungry stomachs after a day of fire and ice. It had started out cold and ended hot. Carrying the heavy packs' mile after mile began to wear. It was truly a testament to our orientation skills to have backtracked the way we did. From above, the Rio Batopilas appeared to be really down compared to last year, which is exactly what we were hoping for. Sure enough, upon down climbing to our river exit point of last year, it was clearly apparent that the river was significantly lower (the agua was cristal). Enough so that we could just stay in the river bed and not have to climb around the perceived "Box of Death." We were able to continue in the river bed, passing through what in reality was the backside of a meander that proved ultra-challenging. No sun penetration into this tight canyon stretch, coupled with two very big swims, had me shivering so violently that I snapped the top off of my lighter in lieu of starting a warming fire. Thank the gods that Dean deals better with the cold water than I do as that Minnesota boy came through with a roaring fire.

"I don't miss cigarettes, but we all get high. Scott loves to drink, and we partake of the herb."

The sheer horror of cold water has always been an unpleasantry that I shied away from. It is a real zen activity to remove what the body experiences from what the mind allows. In the end, as we live a mortal existence, the mind eventually surrenders to the glorious sensations of being alive, even as you feel you will die. At least mine did, and the reality of hypothermia would always rear its ugly head. It was more than an out-of-body experience; this was standing in the flames of mortality. I had brought along a thermometer on this expedition for a more accurate measurement to attach to the statement, "It's cold." I got a reading of 42 degrees Fahrenheit. Ten minutes of that crap, even while wearing a wetsuit, did wonders for my reconnecting with this physical plane of existence. We had another big swim following a rope pack lowering that then necessitated another warming fire. Calories really needed to be constantly consumed.

"Mon. 1/31/94 8:45 am

No Sun coupled with two 'big' swims got me to wondering if I would ever see home again and Alice, who I miss terribly. I am dead serious. After the 1st water series, I needed to start a fire on top of this huge boulder. This being just above our pack lowering approx. 200 ft swim through a dark, deep, still pool. I didn't want to go ever since I was so cold already. The 2nd fire after this swim followed by an even longer swim, at which time I was tapped, almost unable to function at all. My legs stopped kicking, and I feared I would drown in the icy water. Upon emerging, I plopped onto my back with pack & it took approx. 2 min. to muster the strength to stand up! I'm sore head to toe, in body, mind, & soul. We made this campsite by default due to my need for fire! Scott is up for Dinner, and I plan on eating a lot. No Breakfast was a dumb idea. It could have cost me a lot. My life is worth many such meals."

This part of the Barranca Batopilas is very deep, dark, and narrow. To have entered it was really an article of faith, as well as it being a belief. We really needed to have a belief regarding our abilities, especially in light of last year's failure. Failure is of course relative. We accomplished one hell of a push last year, and in fairness to all involved, it was an effort worthy of writing home about. Having faith simply required a spiritual suspension of the laws of probability. With this expedition, we were resupplied and reinvigorated. Having lower water volume helped with furthering not only our resolve, but also our absolute ability and conviction that we could succeed. Not having to contend with precipitation this time around removed any flash flood potential from the list of things that could potentially negate completing this canyon descent. Injury, hypothermia, quicksand, snake bite, and a myriad of other unknowns all played a role in us exercising as much care as we could with our measured movement in the canyon, as this year fatalism had no place at this Round Table of friends.

"Tues. 2/1/94 11:25 am

We passed through the very tight boxy area to the confluence with the A. Diciochi. It is open and sunny here. There are primitive Tara. dwellings behind me. Another push to the A. Hondo confluence which should be just around the next bend. We had to swim through a long, approx. 200 ft. box to get here. I doubt if I could have made it yesterday! Cont. 4:25 pm We passed A. Hondo & it was flowing a good bit, falling in a Cascade approx. 15 ft. high. There was the distinct smell of Sulphur denoting a Hot Spring! Seeps dripped from the side the Arroyo entered on! The Canyon has opened up since the icy box. Camp is situated on an excellent Beach that was actually sunny when we reached it. I was beginning to tire in my legs, although my pack had done the magic weigh less trick! Lots of bouldering and swims today. What a day. I'm tired & famished, but not enough to ignore this is the most amazing Canyon yet seen."

"Weds. 2/2/94 5:00 pm

We put in a very good day today and covered a lot of miles. It was hot & cold depending on if the Sun could penetrate the deep, meandering Canyon. Mostly bouldering with periodic wading. We are just shy of the bend to the N. at the top of which the A. Caliente enters the Rio Batopilas. We are estimating three days to the Bridge if all goes as normal! Pine Trees started creeping into the Arboreal mix once again, and the Palm Trees seemed to disappear. Now they are back, and the Pines are restricted to the rim. High thin cloud covers once again as last night, but it is no longer cold. The Sun has blazed all day, every day, and there is no wind to speak of. All in all, it is perfect weather."

With this canyon we were pushing in, we had begun to feel that we were accomplishing our goal. That made us feel very confident that our style of canyoneering, along with all our experience practicing it, had us on track and poised to pull off a full descent of the canyoneering stretch of the Barranca Batopilas, including the Vertical Vietnam gorge. No bad injuries or sickness, along with all seeming to have very good attitudes, contributed to making a light visible at the end of this canyon tunnel. To reach the Arroyo Agua Caliente required a 400-foot cold pool swim that was exhausting. The amount of time I spent in the water precipitated my usual uncontrollable shivering. I just don't have the body fat for this shit. I am an Ectomorphic Desert Dweller. Thank the gods for warming fires made from an abundant supply of driftwood. Wood was also used for cooking, sterilizing drinking water, and generating light. Very atavistic.

One large enamel pot was the workhorse that served us all. I myself had taken to just drinking the river water straight out of suitable spots. I felt a desire for that level of connection with this reality that certainly could have blown up in my face. The river could be termed sweet water, but Trojan horses come in many guises. Throughout today there were high thin clouds in a canyon that is still very tight. There are multicolored walls. It is incredibly spectacular here. Reaching shy of the Arroyo Rupiachi on this **Thursday** spent expending the energy required to meet this canyon head-on represented a perfectly reasonable goal met for the day.

"*Cont. 4:05 pm*

The camp was pitched a little early due to fatigue and having made just shy of the A. Rupiachi. What a day of it. The Canyon is still tight, with the multicolored walls, choked with Greenery, towering all around.! I should video. Dinner is mine tonight, rice, but with fresh Garlic & Onions. Let me finish my Cocoa/ Coffee mix first. I did take two hard knocks on the legs today. One made me cry out in pain. It was nothing compared to the agony of the swim. This is what will do me in, I fear. I shiver so violently as to be unable to start a fire. My senses get muddled & I just want to be at home, all warm, with my sweet Alice! Death by Barranca, be thy not proud."

"Fri. 2/4/94 4:05 pm

We have camped approx. two mi or so from the Bridge after a long, hard day of it. Today was our longest yet, through nonstop Boulder Field City. No big swims, thankfully! I awoke to rain pelting my Bivy Bag, so I was unable to do the usual sleep & wait for the others to get going. We are off at 9:30, w/o the Rain, and we pushed really hard all day w/o taking many or long breaks, there are increasing signs of habitation, and we came upon our 1st Goat Herd(s). I should treat the water I suppose, due to the Goat, Cow, & Burro Shit. The little Black Biting Bastards have made their appearance. I'm feeling good, except I scraped both my Forearms pretty bad, making a descent! Cont. 6:07 pm Scott made a great Pasta dinner. I was so hungry. This may be the last entry I make in a Journal during an actual Canyon descent. I plan on announcing my retirement after this one. As for the Guaynopa, that will be for someone with the young, wild-eyed spirit I started with back in 1987! So young, so strong, so determined. This trip has broken all that. It has shown that I will be 36 y.o. & that my hips & knees feel it. All the bust-ass trips. How tough, how strong I was. Still am, only hopefully wiser. On the 1st day in the Rio, I thought I would die. Here I am alive, happy to be. Longing for my home, myself!"

"Sat. 2/5/94 8:34 pm

We actually made it to Laguna Aboreachi. The ride out from the Bridge at La Bufa brought us straight here, and it only cost us 20 Pesos for the gas cost! What luck. It was late in the day, after hanging out at the Bridge since 11:30, the time we made the walkout after breaking the camp at 9:30 and following a trail most of the way out. I walked approx. two mi. to La Bufa for Beer & Sodas & later, J. & D. did the same. We met some Americans who owned the house in La Bufa along the road. After chatting a while, Antonio & his Wife came along in their Truck & the rest is history!"

Following the successful conclusion of the epic 2-part descent of the Barranca Batopilas, a feat that most likely was a first, I made my way to Guachochi on a filming expedition, where I wanted to interview the famous human rights activist Edwin Bustillos. He had a radio program on XETARR that exposed issues affecting the Tarahumara Indians. He was a no-show with meeting up with me, as apparently, he was the victim of an assassination attempt. I did finally get the interview a few weeks later in Chihuahua City, all clandestine in my hotel room. I was also in Guachochi to meet up with my girlfriend Alice.

After she arrived, we made our way to the Cascada Gran Salto on the Batopilas, and I rappelled it just for a hoot. From there, we went on around, down to Batopilas, to hike up and over to the village of Urique. While spiked under the stars at Cerro Colorado, two Caballeros came along at 6:00 in the morning. Their riding upon us caused me to sit up. One caballero produced a bottle of tequila from his saddlebag. He threw the cap away and offered me a slug. I declined due to the wee hour of the morning and asked him why he threw the cap away. He said they didn't need it anymore as they galloped off to go up and over to the village of Urique.

On the other side of the immense ridge separating the

Barrancas Batopilas and Urique, we encountered two pot farmers who entered our camp that was situated just above the pueblito of Los Alicos. They were armed. I asked if they were hungry or thirsty. They said no, and then they produced a large wad of newspaper filled with sensimilla buds. They asked if we wanted to smoke. I told them we had no pipe or paper. One of them quickly fashioned a pipe out of a discarded aluminum can. He placed a large bud in the makeshift pipe, and then he reached into the fire to retrieve a lump of coal to place next to it. We all took a hit, and then the pipe maker threw his creation into the fire pit. It was all very ceremonial. They announced their departure and I inquired about the wad of buds they were leaving. We were told it was a present.

After spending some time in Urique, we headed back to New Mexico but returned for a house-sitting gig in Urique at "La Casa Tomas" for the month of April. From Urique, Alice and I had at first made our way to the fishing village of El Colorado. The villagers were once again so gracious and hospitable. My friend Talchito offered us accommodations. We attended a quinceañera, and the women were so pleased to doll Alice up for the festivity. We returned back to Urique, where I celebrated my 36th birthday with a fiesta attended by many new friends. The villagers called me "Gringo Prieto." I spoke to them regarding government plans to build a huge hydroelectric dam down by Temoris that would ultimately inundate their village. They spoke to me about a potential need for revolution. Passing through Chihuahua City had us thirsting for beer. A stop at a cantina had a conversation regarding politics come up. When I told my barstool neighbor I was a communist, he immediately stood bolt upright. I too stood up in anticipation of chingasos. He threw his arms around me while exclaiming, "Comrade!" Turns out it was a communist bar. After that, drinks were not paid for by us. Alice and I attended the cinema where they were showing "Schindler's List." As Alice is Jewish, the poignancy was not lost on me. It was time to head back to New Mexico.

The Storm Surge

My four-year-old daughter Marie wouldn't even come down from the empty parking lot to take a closer look at the ocean. A gray Northern California sky had heralded our arrival at the rough Pacific coast. Her two-year-old brother James waited patiently by a placid creek flowing into the ocean, with a fishing pole stuck diligently out in hopes of landing the big one. We were down from Medford, Oregon, for a week of spring break along the shore of my old childhood playground. Their mother and I had recently divorced, and after this one-week vacation, I would relocate back to New Mexico with the hopes that my children would join me soon.

After the usual mayhem of coordinating the linear movement of two small human beings, we had set out from the parking lot of Dean Martin's beach down to a small creek flowing into the Pacific Ocean. The plan was to fish a bit before retiring back to a Crescent City hotel room. Cartoon Network would round out the day's activities, which had started with a visit to Trees of Mystery. I remembered the area well from my childhood, my father having been stationed at an Air Force Radar Site above the mouth of the Klamath River. Long since closed, it is now part of the Redwood National Park. Nine hundred feet above the Pacific Ocean was such an incredible playground.

For my children, fishing constituted the use of a cut stick fashioned with a line and weighted at the end. Any source of water was a potential fish stomping ground in their young minds. Halfway to the creekbed, Marie bolted back up to the parking lot. No amount of pleading on my part could overcome the power of the Pacific Ocean that she seemed to sense had plans of its own. Large waves crashed 200 feet to our left, the watery foam coming to rest against a cacophonous background. It all seemed like a day at the beach, Northern California style. Just don't get in the frigid water and hope for sunshine.

Stubbornness on my part had dictated that I continue leading little James down to the creek, holding him by his little trusting hand, he with his little fishing pole and I with his sister's pole. I quickly got him situated for some serious angling in the practically dry creek, and I turned to yell encouragement up to Marie to join us for our sporting adventure as she sat mutely on the low wall next to our automobile.

Feeling confident that James had the situation in hand, I jogged back up to retrieve Marie as she exclaimed, "Too scary, Dad!" I slung her giggling, over my shoulder, glancing down with pride in my heart at the vision of my son casting his weighted line into a trusted situation. He glanced ever so slightly in our direction as if to say, "You're burning daylight."

We moved up the creek bed to get away from the loud surf. We could then relax while we fished. I could tell them of my deep love for them. I could try to explain why in one week's time I would be leaving. How it could be a long time before I saw them again. Tell them to be good for their mother. Life's twists and turns were proving difficult for me. Despite desires for a family, a steady job, and the American Dream, I watched as it was all unraveling. The job was there, but the failed American Dream paled in comparison to losing the nuclear family. The fact that my babies no longer slept under my roof all the time provided me the means to work too much and to come home so exhausted that sleep would transport me daily to the dream world where I didn't feel the pain of an exploded family. I could wake and be back at work with no time in between to brood over this horrible situation. I could hang on for my weekends spent with my children. Exhaustion was cleverly hidden, as I wasn't going to let anything more slip away. Time with the kids versus the job. I reached an endpoint. I was leaving. I wanted them with me always, and I struggled to put it all in perspective, feeling I could enter the dream world and stay there forever.

Taking James by the hand, Marie out ahead, we walked along the side of the creek for 100 feet or more. Marie turned to say something, and her eyes threw open real wide in terror. In that split second, I braced, unsure of the reasoning. A wall of cold water slammed into my back. I gripped James' hand tight. We were moving rapidly upstream in a froth of white water. Holding tight to my son and lifting him up high so he wouldn't drown, I focused on grabbing hold of Marie as she kayaked in front of us. I reached and grabbed her with my free hand, and the torrential water wrenched her out of her jacket. I flung her jacket to the side as I held tight to James and I sought to reacquire a grip on Marie as we were being further engulfed in the wave. As we rocketed along, James remained mute. No words of protest or fright came from him as his sister calmly stated, "I'm not having any fun." I finally got hold of her firmly. My instant plan called for a death grip on them both. I needed to be ready for the ensuing outrush of water. I needed to have us all braced against being swept out to sea. My legs frantically searched for rocks large enough to get one of my knees wedged in between them. I managed to turn my body while holding them up high just as the water started racing out. I wedged my knee firmly between two boulders and held on to them tight.

In an instant, the water was gone. We were left drenched in a creek that barely rose above my ankles. As quickly as the water receded, the sensation of extreme cold penetrated my brain along with the cries of my children. Locking them both in my arms, I hurried back to the car and an empty parking lot. We were all alone. None had witnessed our potential demise. Even Highway 101 above the parking lot was devoid of other souls. I wanted to cry out, "A little help here!" Instead of the arrival of any Calvary, I settled into the tasks at hand. Amidst the wailing of Marie and James, I started the car and turned on the heater. Wet clothes were removed and they were both placed in their car seats with a thick goose-down sleeping bag to cover them. I shut the car door to their now quiet voices as I began to shiver violently. I felt numb all over as I retrieved a wet smoke to help calm my nerves. The useless wet smoke disintegrated, and I frantically got a new pack of smokes from the glovebox. The heated car air tempted me to linger. Marie asked me if I was all right and about what had happened. I didn't linger, shutting the car door to have a smoke and shiver like mad. I wasn't going to give myself the luxury of thought, having survived one of the worst experiences of my life. A life that had seen so much.

I have fought wildland fires, been an Emergency Medical Technician on ambulances, wildland fires, and search and rescues. I have done original explorations of remote canyons in Mexico while passing blood and nursing broken ribs. I have clipped treetops while flying in a helicopter. I have rescued injured people from wilderness settings and retrieved the bodies of unfortunate souls. I have known the dead and dying. I have pushed myself through physical pain and endurance to the point of sheer exhaustion. Now my mind was calm as I shivered through a smoke. We were alive. The children, now warmed, cheerfully recounted their adventure as I climbed into the warm car soaking wet for the drive back into Crescent City.

Upon finding a suitably cheap motel, I instructed the kids to wait as I paid for the room with wet bills. The proprietors had greeted my disheveled and wet arrival with a hint of guarded caution, and they listened to my tale of near-death with a marked detachment. Pronouncing that my wet cash was good cash, they gave me the keys to our room. Once in our room, a warm shower put us all even more right. I alternately washed their little bodies while scrubbing our ocean-soaked clothes. While washing myself, inspection revealed my blue and black knee jam. Motrin was taken to help alleviate the swelling and pain. My attempt to put right in my head this life-affirming event was helped by the children recounting the adventure of the big wave. My attempt at any comfort from the motel owners had been stymied by their pragmatic business dealings. My request to machine-wash our ocean-wet clothes had been met with my need to pony-up more money. I called their mother to fess-up to our big misadventure. She was not upset, and even expressed gratitude over their being with me during such a cosmic event. An agreement was reached over not informing my mother regarding the event, as well as a resolution to a tricky money issue that the divorce involved. In speaking with her, I needed to decompress. To share the horror of that moment. I desired comfort beyond pragmatics.

After I prepared a warm meal in our room, Cartoon Network rounded out the day's activities. We all slept well.

In the end, I can't fully explain what happened. I can really only recount the tale. I learned that "sneaker waves" had claimed several lives along the Oregon Coast, drowned, during the same timeframe as our event. After my arrival back in New Mexico, a newspaper article was mailed to me regarding the incidents. My mother, who now knows of our adventure, knows not to use it against my desire to share an adventurous life with my children. The little people I love so much. They are my life. When tasked to adventure, Marie continues to state that the ocean is "too scary."

Chapter 7
Mexico, 2001–2004

The early 2000s presented further possibilities for exploring México. It was a place toward which I had continued to hear the call of adventure. Seeking identity has always had me desirous of learning to speak Spanish. My maternal grandmother spoke only Spanish, and as a child, I couldn't even communicate with her. Despite my mother's L1 being Spanish, she always told me she couldn't remember enough to teach me when I expressed sadness over not being able to talk with my Abuela. The truth is that she had been shamed for being a Spanish speaker. New Mexico became a state of the Union following the great land grab of 1848 and its required abandonment of cultural identity. Speaking Spanish was not only frowned upon by acculturation, it was subjected to derision. I learned Spanish in High School, College, and by throwing myself to the wolves of conversation.

As little boys, my brother and I were set upon by local ruffians in Chama, New Mexico. They gleefully exclaimed, "They're not White and they're not Mexican. Let's beat them up." This was the first time I heard the term "Mexican." My mother referred to us as Spanish. I went on to learn that "Mexican" was considered a dirty word. When I brought home a Spanish wife, my mother finally dropped, saying we were Spanish in favor of saying "Hispanic." My mother always hated when I said I am half Mexican. Studying science and history has helped edify me that my mother's people have Native American blood mixed with Iberian. I am a Coyote. A Mestizo. A mongrel and outsider. I love the people, food, and topography of México, and I decided to self-identify as Mexican. This resulted from never feeling accepted by either the White or the Hispanic worlds.

Copper Canyon country became a strange attractor that satisfied inclusion along with an exclusion from all humanity found in its boundless wilderness possibilities. Solitude with a sense of belonging. The proximity of New Mexico to the Mexican state of Chihuahua easily lent itself to more trips down South. Leaving New Mexico to live in Oregon had taken me far afield of a very large backyard, but Y2K had brought me back to the high desert where I belong. As I was very comfortable with the nuances of travel in México, and I desired to see and experience more, only a lack of imaginative dreaming could hold me back. The Sierra Madre Mountains hold so many treasures that I could never see them all. Life is nowhere near long enough to accommodate visiting the myriad potential destinations. Even a thousand lifetimes could not realize that goal.

Barranca Guaynopa, 2001

Moving to Crownpoint, New Mexico, had me alighting on the high desert Navajo Nation with my girlfriend Martha, where she was a nurse for the Indian Health Service and I was courting the potential of teaching science at Crownpoint Institute of Technology (Navajo Technical University). We had a long spring break potential of heading down south to Mexico to attempt a descent of the Barranca Guaynopa. It had been a back-burner dream of mine for years to have a go at this great giant horseshoe barranca formed by the Rio Sirupa. The river descends through a series of gorges (Huapoca, Esmeralda, Multi-colored, and Guaynopa). The trip generated buzz amongst the Diné when Martha had shared photos depicting the poverty under which the Tarahumara and Pima Indians lived. They held a collection drive, and before we could fully comprehend their level of concern, we had several large Hefty bags of donated clothing to take with us down to Mexico to distribute to the Pima Tribe.

Approaching the "Veintiocho" Immigration Stop is when it came to me that spontaneous relief efforts were frowned upon by the Mexican government and the clothes would most likely be confiscated. When I was asked by the border guard what was in the bags, my response of "clothes" seemed to satisfy his curiosity, and we were waved through. The trip down to Madera was magical and filled with beer drinking as we explored a part of Mexico that was unknown to me. We pushed many dirt roads in the mountains in search of where the Buffalo roam. We came upon some campesinos who were broken down and we were able to render them aid. Our arrival out of the blue in the middle of nowhere had them fairly mesmerized.

The first night in Mexico was spent by an abandoned hacienda straight out of the *Blair Witch Project*. It had been raining the whole way down as we made our way to Madera. I had a sinking feeling that this didn't bode well for our canyon plans. Madera is an interesting mountain town where Martha and I were immediately befriended by a woman clerk at the local hardware store. She invited us to dine that evening with her family. Afterward Martha and I went to a local disco to dance, where I was subjected to a weapons check at the door. Later, at a quaint lounge, I was approached by a young man asking me if I knew a gentleman he was pointing at. When I told him I had no idea, he said that the man was the governor and that the governor wanted to buy us drinks. We more than gladly took the government official up on his offer and proceeded to have a lovely time. I asked the governor why the Pima Indians were left to starve. He said it was because the Mexican people were blind to them. I told him of the sadness in my heart over this situation affecting all the tribes of Mexico. He sympathized and said, "What's to be done?"

When the conversation turned to what we were up to in their beautiful country, the governor expressed major concern. He proceeded to relay tales of how people were continually drowning in the river, and he implored us to just be tourists and not attempt our planned insane itinerary. I was fairly buzzed and adamant that we would stick with our game plan, so he asked us to come by his office the next morning as he could contact a gringo rancher who lived at the canyon bottom. He said the rancher would be able to advise us on if the river was in flood. Agua Negra would spell the end of our canyon dream. The next morning, I was able to speak to the rancher via radio, and sure enough, he reported the river was flooding. He invited us to come to visit and have a look-see ourselves.

The day was spent in Madera trying to figure out what to do with the donated clothes. It came upon me to approach the local Catholic priest for advice. It meant sitting through Mass while we waited for an opportunity to speak with him. As Martha and

I were both raised Catholic, we knew the drill. I, as a lapsed Catholic atheist, felt armed with a confident resolve to get this clothing donation accomplished. In speaking with the priest, I made the origin of the clothing known. I made it clear that the clothes were to go only to the Pima Indians. Indian to Indian. He agreed to take half the bags, and I would take the other half to the canyon bottom in hopes of more directly distributing them.

The next day we took the precipitous drive to the canyon bottom through the pouring rain. Along the way, we were tasked to pull a large toppled tree out of the way. The rancher and his wife ran a religious camp at the canyon bottom. They were gracious enough to invite us to stay in a guest house as well as to attend a dinner party that was being held that evening. Martha and I hiked the river bottom to the bridge above Agua Termales de Huapoca, the theoretical start of our canyoneering descent. At the Puente Huapoca, the river was roaring with Agua Negra. The floating logs indicated that the river was still rising. It was a no-go. It would have been suicide to enter the river. Agua Termales was being developed into quite the aquatic park, and it served as a juxtaposition to the wilderness gorges that lay ahead. The rancher relaid a tale of how some "Back to the Earth" squatters had laid claim to the Huapoca Hot Springs land. The Army and gunfire settled that dispute, and now people can go to Mexican Disneyland. Dinner that evening was attended by many church officials, and the conversation included a fascination with our atheistic clothing drive, our intended expedition plans, and my biocentrism. Later, Martha and I met with a Pima Indian ranch hand who graciously took possession of the Navajo clothing for distribution with his people.

The river flooding dictated we head to the Barranca del Cobre to check on the feasibility of descending the lower half of that canyon. A detour was first taken to the village of Maguarichi and Piedras del Lumbre. That evening, there was a dance held at the lodge we had found accommodations at. It was a lively affair, and many people were in attendance. It took Martha and me very little time to attract attention as we didn't observe the custom of waiting to start to dance until the song had played a little while. Normally with the first note, we were off to the races. We were forgiven for our faux pas as we quickly learned the proper etiquette. Beer, wine, and tequila all flowed liberally.

The next day we made our way to Piedras del Lumbre, a wonderland situated a few miles outside of Maguarichi where geysers shoot hot water into the sky. Apparently, this whole area has major hot water aquifers. A gold mine up the road was abandoned because the pumps could not prevent it from flooding with scalding water. Village picnics included placing prepared chicken carcasses into boiling pools to cook.

When we arrived at the Divisadero, I was able to borrow some binoculars and ascertain that the Rio was agua cristal. We were able to descend the steep Areponapuchi trail where, along the way, Martha fell three times, and in tears, she confessed to the arduous nature of what we were doing. Five wonderful river days saw beautiful weather, and two strong and willing spirits made a successful descent of the lower Barranca del Cobre.

We encountered a large Coatimundi band traveling on the opposite side of the Rio Urique. Due to their potential of being a cantankerous bunch, I was glad they were on the other side of the river. One evening we witnessed an extended Tarahumara family come down to the opposite side of the river from us. They quickly started a very large roaring fire that lit up the canyon bottom, and they were then able to efficiently conduct their settling down for the evening activities. And then equally as quick, the canyon went dark, and they quietly settled in for the night. This ethnographic event didn't really negate the "white man" fire stereotyping as it was positively utilitarian and logical in nature on their part. The Tarahumara have a fear of a creature that inhabits the rivers. Supposedly, in the past, crocodiles were found in the Rio Fuerte up to Témoris. The Rarámuri also speak of "river voices." I did hear these "voices" several times in the night on this trip. I have only ever heard them while in the Barranca del Cobre, never on the Barranca Sinforosa or Batopilas. They are like a muffled conversation heard just out of earshot that occurs only on certain stretches of the river.

The last day canyoneering had us leaving the Arroyo Hondo confluence quite early as we desired to really hump it and make the village of Urique after entering the Barranca Urique. As I had an injured back, we totally neglected to visit the large amphitheater that I had encountered along the stretch back in 1991. Hell, we didn't even see it. The nose-to-the-grindstone thinking was that we could hitch a ride the last 5 miles into town once we reached the start of the road at Guadalupe Coronado. Sadly, there was not a ride to be had. The one and only car in town was a sad and broken-down affair. We had run out of cigarettes. The call of a hot shower and a bed grew ever louder the closer we got to Urique as I agonized with my aching back. We straggled into Urique at 10:00 pm, and as our dismay encountered all the tiendas being closed, we soldiered on. A very odd fellow intercepted us and said he knew of a good place where we could sleep. We followed him along with winding ways until he reached a shack where he kicked the door in. We bowed out gracefully from his presence and found that the sleeping owners of the Hotel Cañón were more than glad to arise and rent us a room. Martha got up early the next morning and went for coffee and cigarettes. At that specific moment in time, she was my hero.

We had had a wondrous trip filled with measured arduousness. It had been a great opportunity to field-test a large canyoneering backpack prototype I had designed. The pack performed wonderfully. Much better than my injured back.

2001 Barranca Urique

My children and I desired a Mexican Christmas adventure, so my son James and I gathered our fortitude and headed south off the Navajo Nation. Teaching college science for Navajo Technical University was professionally rewarding, but the isolation of being a single father on the reservation was proving to be a challenge of a different sort. As I had broken up with Martha, my reason for living in the Navajo Nation, I felt the resurgence of wanderlust. My 3-year-old son James lived with me, and his 5-year-old sister Marie lived with their mother in Silver City. James attended preschool in the Navajo Nation. I was called in for a parent/teacher conference where the take-away came down to him not being Navajo. Neither was I. Though I had long hair when I moved to Crownpoint, I had cut it short to interview with the University. The last question they had of me at the interview was why I had cut my hair. The interview committee said it didn't matter when I told them my reasoning for doing so. The Diné villagers had become fascinated to know what tribe I came from. Though I am 17% Native American, such knowledge is lost to me by the passage of time. When I wore a gifted Yakima ball cap, they were satisfied with me being Yakima. I let my son's teacher know there was nothing I could do about him not being Navajo.

James and I left Crownpoint in a snowstorm to meet up with Marie in Albuquerque. We boarded the bus for Truth or Consequences. Two days were spent at the River Bend Hot Springs before we shouldered our packs for the 4-mile hike to where we could catch a US Border-bound Mexican limousine bus. Once in El Paso, we were able to walk into Mexico easy enough. What proved impossible was obtaining visas for our entry into the Mexican interior. The children's mother had neglected to give me a notarized permission letter allowing me to take the kids into Mexico. As it was perfectly acceptable to be in Juarez without a visa, we set up siege on the wall preventing our entry. Over the next couple of days, we tried every border crossing station. No amount of sob storying or bribery was met with any success. A visit to the American Consulate proved equally unfruitful. I was growing weary of the chase, spending good money after bad. I confabulated the existence of vampires in Juarez as Marie and James had grown weary of all the walking we were doing. They advocated a preference for taxi rides. As my wallet preferred walking, I convinced them that vampires would come out when the sun went down, so we needed to hoof it fast back to our hotel room. They really picked up the pace while relaying their knowledge set regarding creatures of the night.

We gave up on Juarez and retreated to El Paso, where I had friends who could prove very helpful. I was able to forge a permission letter and get it notarized. We then took the bus to the border crossing into Palomas, Mexico, where obtaining visas was a breeze. From there, we were able to bus to Chihuahua City, and from there, we could ride the train to Bahuichivo. It was then easy enough to shuttle down to the village of Urique, where we were able to pass a pleasant Christmas at Casa Tomas. I was able to purchase Marie and James bunches of toys at a village tienda. These were hidden until Christmas morning, further solidifying their belief that Santa could find you anywhere. Micah True (Caballo Blanco) showed up in Urique, having run over from Batopilas. He passed Christmas with the kids and me at Casa Tomas, which had filled up with a bunch of Canadian tourists. Micah impressed me with his night vision as we navigated the village at night. He was unimpressed with my canyoneering exploits and cajoled me to become a runner like him. I pointed out that while I could run, I favored walking. There was a Christmas Eve party being held in the main house, and I was excited to attend. Micah wanted to partake of the herb first, so we got good and baked before we would theoretically make our grand entry. However, once altered, introspective Caballo Blanco wanted nothing to do with such frivolity. My desire was to see pretty Canadian women, and Micah wanted to seek doors of perception.

Barranca Del Cobre, May 2002

My mind was made up to leave the Navajo Nation once the school year ended. I loved teaching Chemistry and Biology to the Diné student body at Navajo Technical University, but it was time for manifesting wanderlust. I had started out lecturing my students with the standard transmission style of edification, but the lack of engagement I perceived that was occurring in my classes caused me to stop talking and write two words on the whiteboard. "Reductionism" and "Eurocentrism." I then defined the words. I also explained how the Diné were neither. I apologized for my misstep and further elaborated on our task at hand. They needed to absorb "Western" scientific knowledge in order to pursue their varied career choices. I needed to adapt. After all was made clear, I was freed up to deliver the scientific body of knowledge in my ever-evolving style of doing things. When I ascertained that they were not reading their textbooks (they claimed they only understood the material when I explained it), I was off to the races.

Finally, the way humans should learn was a door opened before me. They respected me for being a wildland firefighter and explorer. One of my students had a grandfather who was a Shaman. He reported to me that his grandfather had a vision of me. His grandfather told him that I didn't know more than he did but that I did know how to explain things the way white people want it understood. The grandfather told his grandson he should listen to me. I was invited to speak regarding the anthrax scare as the Post Office was a major social hub. It was a talk that involved the fear of honey. Another occasion had me speaking on the juxtaposition of science and technology. I gave another poignant talk about smallpox-tainted blankets in relationship to thoughts of civic duty following the 911 terrorist attack. The Diné became convinced I could interpret dreams. I could not.

Shortly before the school year came to an end, I received a phone call out of Washington State asking if I would guide a group down in the Barranca del Cobre. I was off to a different race. Plans were set to meet up with part of the group in Truth or Consequences at the Riverbend Hot Springs. My great friend Bryan from the 1993 Barranca Batopilas expedition showed up to see me off. When Cristal and two men party members arrived, Bryan immediately predicted trouble. Sadly, he kept his premonition to himself. Cristal was beautiful and obviously not otherwise engaged as she and I did that magnetic thing that cannot be contrived.

We made our way to El Paso in order to meet the other canyoneering group participants. The night was spent at a hotel near the El Paso Airport, where I elected to sleep in the van we had arrived in, as I was not up to the level of drunken and stoned revelry that the Washington cabal wanted to engage in. Cristal liked my option and a die got cast as she joined me in the van. Four men and three women breezed across the border for a descent of the lower Barranca del Cobre, a trip that I had just done the previous year. It was not an Earth-shattering endeavor. We made our way to Areoponapuchi by bus with Cristal wanting me to manifest an "I would keep her safe" way of being. She slept peacefully on my lap.

The descent was made difficult by the overbearing heat of the month of May. The initial drop into the canyon had me realizing that these were not my friends and I was becoming dispirited by the whole experience. I wanted the group to camp down low where we could safely have the kind of fire the group would surely want to have. We also stood a chance of locating huecos where we could water up before the hot, steep, long, and final descent to the canyon bottom. The group did not want to heed my advice and opted to push onward to the crossing dropoff ridge. The ridge being windswept and exposed represented the exact wrong place to start a large campfire. No watering up could occur with this plan. I felt a failure as a guide. I knew this was one large mistake on my part. The group wanted to hoot and holler, drink tequila, get stoned, and definitely not engage in a quiescent canyon experience respectful of being in the land of the Tarahumara. I wanted to sleep off separate from the group, and Cristal elected to do likewise.

The next day saw major fracturing as their alpha male proceeded to come at me with his best shot of me being too articulate. As I carried a large hunting knife, I felt no fear of them as he relayed how they didn't like me monopolizing Cristal's affection. I had decided to cut ties and just accompany the group to the canyon bottom, at which point I would bid them adieu. They could not possibly get lost, as all they needed to do was stay in the fucking canyon bottom until they reached the village of Urique. As it was not a paying guiding gig, I felt freed up to dictate what my spiritual limitation was. I told Cristal of my plan, and she tearfully told me she couldn't abandon her friends. They crossed the river, and I did not. On parting, I told Cristal I would go around to meet them in Urique, and with a kiss, we parted ways. That evening she sat on the other side of the Rio Urique and waved at me as the river was too loud to allow communication.

The next day's climb out was made very interesting by the blazing sun. All I needed was to make the top without running out of water and succumbing to heat sickness. My lifelong fascination with death by exposure played errant thoughts through my attempts at Zen posturing silence. Along the way, when I stopped to enjoy a cigarette, a Tarahumara Campesino came along and asked to bum a smoke from me. We silently sat, relaxed, and enjoyed our respite under a shade tree. With our tobacco smoked, he rose to leave and inquired about the rest of the group. I told him how we had parted ways. He told me I was better off without them. The blazing heat had me concerned about the reality I had just experienced. It was as if it was a door of perception that opened on what I wanted to hear. The top got reached. Cold beers got drunk. Cigarettes worked their calming magic. The night got spent in a comfortable bed. Exhausted, I slept the sleep of the dead.

I made my way by train to Bahuichivo, where I was able to hook up with a shuttle ride down to Urique. Five days were spent in the hot canyon bottom waiting on a Cristal that never arrived. I painted a welcome sign for La Casa Tomas for my friend Chema, the poet. As there were three partners involved in the property, and Chema was the only one in residency at the time, a decision had been made to call the place "Entre Amigos" instead of using Tomas, Keith, or Chema. I walked into town and purchased black and white paint. Then I melted in the sun while painting a sign welcoming tourists. Sitting outside a village market while enjoying a smoke, a pretty schoolgirl was goaded by her girlfriends to approach me and do a pirouette. Her marimba's long and graceful legs topped by white panties were revealed by the twirling of her skirt. In that moment of my loneliness, she giggled and ran off.

After five days, I realized something must have happened to delay the Washington group. I made my way to Creel to inquire regarding them. No one had seen or heard of them. The next day the Washington group arrived via rail from Bahuichivo. I was so excited to see Cristal. As she wouldn't even speak with me, I had to ascertain the story of her getting sick on the trek down to Urique from a third party. Her being sick ground their descent to a halt, but they were finally able to make it through. As I was now a persona non grata, the next day, I boarded a Chihuahua City-bound bus to get as much distance as possible between me and them. Between her and me. I grew angrier and angrier over this fucked-up turn of events, and I desired solitude. The Washington crew boarded the same bus as I, and a discomforting multi-hour trip deposited us all to go our separate ways in downtown Chihuahua City.

I checked into a hotel room and then proceeded to go out and get super drunk. I moved from bar to bar looking for a place to happen. I walked down narrow side streets courting disaster while carrying my large hunting knife strapped to a fanny pack. Getting no engagement, my seething anger turned inward. I was really fucking pissed at myself and with heart-on-my-sleeve stupidity. I returned to my hotel room, but the call of the street and smoke had me stepping outside of the hotel lobby. An attractive girl approached and asked to bum a smoke. After a brief leading chat, she asked if I wanted to go with her.

I told her I had a room in the hotel and there was no need to go anywhere. She told me that she wasn't allowed in the hotel. I, charged with self-loathing, said fuck it as I accompanied her to a textbook seedy brothel that smelled of burnt semen. It was all so pathetically symbolic. After business got contracted, and I got on my way, I felt satiated of any anger. Anger at myself. Anger with not understanding women, or more accurately, my angry reaction to not understanding them. Anger with anything un-life-fulfilling.

The morning had my common denominator self experiencing a pseudo-cathartic awakening that revealed a clearer vision of how I had had enough. While not proclaiming celibacy, I did open my eyes wide to the avoidance of entanglement in dreams of requited love. I consumed a lot of coffee to muster the wherewithal to board a bus headed for home.

Barrancas Oteros and Del Cobre, July 2002

The events of the previous May had provided a needed kick in the pants that was long overdue, and I retired to a quiet existence living in a travel trailer park in Las Cruces, New Mexico, where I could work on self-reflection. I worked as a carpenter handyman, and I was freed up to pursue my dreams of being an artist. Marie and James were able to come to stay with me every other week in a Gypsy trailer lifestyle. It was so comfortably snug and kept afloat only by my effort. We had satellite TV. I was neither dependent nor entangled with anyone, and I liked it that way.

July had us launch a multi-week escape down south of the border, which was only 50 miles away. This time I was armed

159

with a permission letter provided by Roberta, the mother of my children Marie and James. It made entry into Mexico a cinch. Roberta made me promise to keep our children safe. They loved to travel, and trains and buses were always a big hit. We bussed to San Juanito, just north of Creel. Creel, the jumping-off point for the Barranca del Cobre, was not our destination. We were headed for Maguarichi on the falda of the Barranca Oteros. As I had been there before I knew we could comfortably settle into a stay at the little lodge Martha and I had stayed at the year before. Unable to find the lodge owner, we passed a clandestine night in the lodge before taking up residency at La Casa Lucero. Doña Lucero was more than willing to rent us a room in her house for a week-long stay. Meals included. She insisted we owed the absent lodge owner nothing, and as she was a local mover and shaker, I figured it was a sociopolitical thing.

From the safety of her abode, we could explore this incredible locale situated on the rim of the great Barranca Otero. We walked everywhere. We hung out and ate at Vicky's restaurant, where there were young children and satellite TV. We explored everywhere. We found a great waterfall where we could swim. Marie made friends with a chicken. Thermal pools were just up the road. Piedras del Lumbre were up another road. We checked on a property we fantasized about moving into. It was complete with an orchard. Little Marie fell through a cattle guard grate with no lasting damage beyond a bunch of stricken wailing. Her accidentally killing a turkey chick had a bit longer-lasting effect that followed her tears.

I had a dream of clowns, so I was not surprised when the next day, a clown troupe arrived in town. This caused quite the stir in the predominantly Catholic village of Maguarichi, as the troupe was a decidedly non-Catholic group of gringo missionaries bent on proselytizing. Doña Lucero felt that Satan himself had arrived to provide entertainment, as entry to see the clown show required listening to their brand of preaching. The show elicited so much entertainment enjoyment amongst all the children in attendance. Marie and James clapped their hands and stomped their feet. As the show admission was free, I deemed it a scant price to pay, hearing how I was going to Hell. At the conclusion of the show, I approached the lead proselytizer to report my atheistic prognostication. He was sufficiently freaked out enough to drop any attempts at saving my soul.

Upon leaving Maguarichi, we made our way to Creel in a pickup that came along with a dead squirrel already hitching a ride in the truck bed. Its corpse sliding back and forth as we traveled the winding road allowed for a morbid game of tag that provided an hour's worth of entertainment. In Creel, we fairly quickly befriended Mag and Mao. Magdalena was from Poland, and Maurizio was from Italy. They had an apartment where we were welcomed to camp on the floor. From their apartment, we were able to stage many day trips exploring the surrounding countryside. I gifted them a pipe carved from beautiful madron wood that resides in Poland to this day. We cooked dinners together. I was able to put together a righteous Irish stew utilizing my grandmother's recipe. As Marie and James showered, Maurizio came to me and asked, "Russell, what does this mean, don't look at our privacy?" We all hitched a ride in a pickup bound for parts further south. Most importantly, they would pass by our intended destination of Puente Umira. The fact that the pickup drove like a bat out of Hell just intensified the excitement.

When we stopped at a small tienda for sodas, I commented on a beautiful Datura meteloides in full bloom. A teacher who had come over to the tienda from the elementary school for lunch relayed a tale of the school children sampling the Jimson weed sap. That precipitated a psychotropic alkaloid-induced rodeo maelstrom. A massive rainstorm broke out a short while after reaching the bridge at Umira, and we had to seek shelter in a large cave where we could start a fire. As too much time passed waiting for a ride, we decided to enter one of the boarded-up chantes to seek better shelter. Just as we gained entry into one of the shacks, a vehicle came along. We flagged them down, and the women occupants immediately set to drying my kids off. The women flagged down another vehicle while relaying an edict to take us, poor creatures, back into Creel.

Once back in Creel, I took Marie and James out to eat at a restaurant. I did our usual thing of ordering food only for them, as I would just eat the more than ample leftovers. Seeing this, a large family seated next to us enjoying a lively dinner occasion sent their teenage son over to say that his mother wanted to buy us dinner. When I told him we already had dinner, he looked so disappointed. Shortly after, he sat back down plate after plate of food began arriving at our table. As we had eaten and we were full, I asked the mesero to box the untouched "leftovers." When we got up to leave, I went over and thanked the mother for kindly sending us food. Immediately outside the restaurant, we encountered a large Tarahumara family asking to be fed. We were able to hand over several plastic bags filled with takeout containers of food. They looked so shocked, bewildered, and appreciative.

Leaving Creel, we made our way to El Colorado, the fishing village at the mouth of the Rio Fuerte. I knew that my friend Talchito would have open arms. Sure enough, Talchito and his wife took us in. As they had three children of their own, I shopped accordingly for groceries to offset our intrusion. The bathing situation was of fascination to Marie and James. It consisted of a three 5-gallon bucket system of getting clean. Marie asked me why we didn't have such a cool setup. The villagers were excited about my return, this time with the children in tow. The fishermen wanted to take James on a fishing run out to the Pacific Ocean with the understanding that I was not to accompany them. I was to trust them. He boarded the fishing boat and excitedly bid me adieu. The woman took Marie and dolled her up in a beautiful red dress. They elaborately braided her hair. Placed on display, she was immediately set upon by a rooster. Falling backward into a rose bush had the thorn scratching give the impression of a savaging. That gallo was caldo that evening. The kids got invited to a birthday party where the busting of the candy-filled piñata resulted in Marie and James enduring a tear-filled dusting up that yielded no candy. The mothers confiscated a share of the piñata booty to give to them and dry their tears. A scene from "Night of the Iguana" saw mothers bringing their young daughters over one by one on a social call as I lounged in a hammock trying to read. It was all so poignantly sweet.

The fisherman had made a record haul of shrimp, and that evening's dinner presented us with as many Camarones as we could eat. Talchito was appointed to take the shrimp haul into

Los Mochis to get top auction dollars for the catch. The bidding resulted in a hefty profit to be shared back in El Colorado. Before leaving Los Mochis, Talchito told me we would make a stop first. Pulling up at a gated hacienda complete with machine gun-toting henchmen had me doing the mental gymnastics required of such situations. Talchito told me to just wait in the car for him. When he passed through the guarded gate, I lounged on the hood and had a smoke. Once back, Talchito explained that he had scored cocaine for the village fisherman. This was evidenced by the large package he had carried out. He further elaborated that he had told "El Jefe" I was an American pistolero that he had brought along for insurance purposes. My brain was racked with thoughts of how this had all gone too far. Talchito laying out plans of how we go into this lucrative business together had my mind racing, thinking of how it was time to bow out.

Back in Los Mochis, my favorite hotel was all booked. We walked a few blocks to another hotel, where the manager reported they were also full. I asked him if Marie and James could wait in his lobby while I checked on yet another place. He agreed, and I headed down the street, hopeful of securing a room. A cop car screeched to a halt alongside me, and a machine gun-toting cop quickly emerged. He sprinted over and shoved me against the wall with the machine gun. I long ago learned to never speak Spanish in these types of situations. I told him I was an American, and I asked him what they wanted with me. He got back in their car, telling his partner, "Esta Americano". Heart racing, I returned to get Marie and James. When the manager inquired if I had found a room, and I told him what had transpired, he miraculously had a room come available for us. I told Marie and James what had happened.

After settling into our room, we went out to see the sites and get a bite. At an open-air Mercado, the same cops that rousted me were there on foot patrol. I slyly pointed them out to the kids. Marie immediately charged up to them, wagging her finger and yelling that I was a good man and to leave her father alone. Clothes for the trip home got washed that evening using the shower stomp technique. At least I could provide them with this nostalgic level of technology.

When we arrived by bus in Chihuahua City, James was in tears, stricken with a need for the restroom. The restroom on the bus was "No sirve". I was really in need of retrieving our luggage from beneath the bus before it took off again. As I couldn't take them across the busy bus terminal to the coin-operated baños, I gave Marie monero and strict instructions to take her stricken and crying brother straight to the restroom and then return directly back to me. I was able to get our baggage from beneath the bus and go looking for them. When they weren't at the restroom, I started to freak out. As I frantically backtracked in search of them, they came along being hand-held by a terminal security guard who admonished me to be more careful with my children.

Barranca Urique, 2003

Spring break was scarcely a temporal consideration for me as I worked as a long-haired handyman carpenter in Las Cruces, New Mexico. My fellow-laborers chided me as being the "Rock Star." As Marie and James were enrolled in school, they did need a spring break block of free time to allow for a canyon sojourn. Plans were set in motion to tie in with my brother John Willow and his son Ben for a father-children Urique trip. My Gypsy trailer was designated as the meet-up point, and I had arranged for a ride that would take us all to the border. The plans fell through when my brother got word to me that he couldn't make it. Feeling somewhat dejected, Marie, James, and I loaded into our arranged ride to El Paso.

Another friend named John (Etue) screeched to a halt in our trailer court to report that my brother John was on his way and that we were to wait for him and his son. They didn't take long to arrive, and we were successfully shuttled to the border. Obtaining visas proved interesting as both John and I had neglected to pay for exit stamping the last times we had been in Mexico. I solved the problem with the $5.00 I offered the official for a stamping. John, however, offered $40.00 for the same consideration. This capital outlay would come back to bite him, plus my having paid five dollars really didn't sit well with his competitive edge. It was a one-upmanship brother kind of thing. Live and learn was the pain-in-the-ass sage wisdom I imparted on him. Visas obtained, we made our bus connections no problem.

The plan was to spend a night at Margarita's place in Creel and then board the "El Chepe" train bound for Bahuichivo. I was sitting in the little patio area at Margarita's reading a book when a beautiful young woman came walking through headed for the dining room. She paused for a brief moment and looked right through me. Later, after dinner, John came to me relaying how he had met some women from Spain, and we should convince them to travel with us. I pointed out to John how this was a father-children trip and not a skirt-chasing extravaganza. He wouldn't relent, so I agreed to speak with them.

Sonia, not only being the beautiful one who looked through me, was amongst this group of five women, four of whom were from Spain, Sonia included. Their American friend Angela was a Santa Fe Public School counselor down for spring break with her Spanish teacher friends: Sonia, Pepa, Lucia, and Eva. They had all been recruited to help with the growing bilingual teacher need occurring in Santa Fe. I spoke to them of our plans to descend to the village of Urique and of the canyon country in general. They were impressed with my knowledge of the area, and they expressed a desire to accompany us. I agreed to them coming with us. Part of my reasoning was my apparent attraction to Sonia and how I had perceived her looking right through me. As I was 45 and I surmised her to be 21, I figured I could let the age difference between us keep me in check. It could be a vicarious proximity alert. I didn't affect aloofness. It was genuine on my part.

Marie and James were so excited. They loved the train, especially the cafe car. Riding the rail afforded the possibility for enjoying a smoke between the rail cars. Sonia came and joined in on the conversation and a smoke. She was obviously highly intelligent and educated. When I detected her interest in my hippie countenance, and I ascertained she was 27 and not 21, I felt freed up to naturalistically let this passion play play itself out. The excitement was palpable amongst us all.

The always exciting shuttle ride down into the Barranca Urique included a brief stop at the beautiful Cerocahui Mission to purchase a case of their delicious vino tinto. The children, John, and I made our way to "Entre Amigos" but not before situating the girls at the Hotel Cañon. Plans were made to meet for dinner at Restaurante Zuelma. The arrival of the Spanish women had created quite a stir in the village, and the restaurant got fairly packed with inebriated local men. Sonia had taken the initiative to save a seat for me next to her. The Spanish girls had been secretly calling me a filthy hippie in jest. Lucia admonished them that I smelled better than they all did. And besides, my nipple was pierced. Also, I could be forgiven any sticks in my hair as it was so salvaje. Sonia apparently let them all know to stay away from the pinche hippie. When some borracho Mexican men started speaking in terms of the pinche Gringos monopolizing the Españolas, Sonia and the other Spanish girls were quick to admonish them.

The next day's plans were to picnic on a river playa up the canyon where awesome swimming holes existed. Sonia accompanied Marie, James, and me when I wanted to move to a less raucous hangout spot. The time spent separately was so magically incredible as we discussed literature, cinema, and all manner of things. When Marie and James scaled a rock wall, Sonia refocused my distracted attention on what they were doing, and I made them get their asses down. The walk back into town had us still separate from the main group. When we overshot the suspension bridge leading back into town, we were faced with a wading of the river. Sonia didn't desire to get her feet wet, so the option was to backtrack to the bridge. I broached the feasibility of giving her a piggyback ride across, and she climbed on board as I very gingerly maneuvered across the river while monitoring the chest-high water efforts of Marie and James. They called out excitedly that they were OK as I remained ever mindful that performing a river dumping with Sonia on my back could fairly scuttle any potential of a continuance of the passion play.

Dinner that evening was a group effort cooked at Entre Amigos. Spaghetti, garlic toast, salad, and vino tinto were enjoyed in a farewell celebration of the girls' departure in the morning. The borrachos showed up at the Entre Amigos gate to drunkenly serenade the Españolas. When it came time for them to leave, they expressed reticence due to the drunkards, so John and I accompanied them back into town along the very dark dirt road. I really needed to resist taking Sonia by the hand as we walked along. I so wanted her to not leave. We parted with hugs all around. 6:00 am had a morning rousting as Sonia had forgotten her gaffas. She came in whispering hello and retrieving her glasses, waving up at me as I lay with Marie and James in the loft. As we had previously exchanged email addresses, she left me with the potential of us reconnecting back in New Mexico.

The return home to New Mexico required me to loan my short-on-cash brother John money. We paid for our passport exit stampings and made our way to Silver City, where John and Roberta (the kids' mother) both lived. Sitting in the Buffalo Bar, John said to me if I could get the pretty barmaid to go home with me, I would be his hero. I exclaimed to the whore-dog that I only had Sonia on the mind. I did get the pretty girl's phone number to shut John up.

Two weeks went by of leaving the ball in Sonia's court before she emailed me to come up to Santa Fe to visit her. I met up with her at the Cowgirl Bar and began a passionate love affair that would culminate in us marrying the following year. Our son Dario was born a year later. Our son Ruben a year after that. Living in Las Cruces had me applying to be a chemist for the City of El Paso. I had taken a lengthy and difficult written exam that I did quite well on. That got me an interview. I figured I needed to clean up my act, cut my hair, and buy new clothes. When I told Sonia of my plan, she implored me not to cut my hair, and I knew that no amount of dressing up and tying my hair back would yield Texas interviewing success. As I had already been picked up to be a crew member on a BLM Fire Engine out of Socorro, New Mexico, I wasn't too concerned. When Sonia asked me what I would do if I wasn't destined to be an El Paso chemist, I told her I would fight fires.

She came to live with me in Socorro the first month of summer, where she got a crash course in something that Spain had no cultural analog of. I had a fire crew, and when we went to the rough and tumble Capitol Bar to engage in nonsense, she could dress as scantily as she wanted. Nobody was going to fuck with her. The insanity of my chosen profession really hit home when I got to briefly return to our apartment from fighting a fire so she could administer eye drops for me. I had really smoked them up on a raging Sacaton grass fire that I needed to return to for an upcoming shift. At the end of that season, she really desired for me to give up on such a dangerous profession and just become a public school teacher like her. I loved fighting fires, but as I loved her more, it was a foregone conclusion. The cosmic ordainment of coupling with Sonia was validated to me by her fellow Spaniards, who reported that she had acted as a woman possessed with an intrepid need to experience Copper Canyon. A canyon that has transcended mere thought and has moved in to inhabit my soul.

Barranca Urique, 2004

Marrying Sonia was a sweet declaration that was followed by us heading to Mexico for a honeymoon spent with Marie and James in tow. Crossing the border at Juarez was a farcical scene as the Mexican limousine bus we boarded in Albuquerque was required to stop in Juarez at the La Migra checkpoint. Expecting we were going to be put through the entry process required to receive visas, we exited the bus and were instructed to stand in an orderly line where a red and green stop and go setup dictated how we were to proceed. When it came to our turn, the green light signaled us to simply reboard the Chihuahua City-bound bus.

Arriving in the city a couple of hours before the departure of "El Chepe" (Chihuahua al Pacifico), the passenger train that would take us on our adventure-bound honeymoon, we had a couple of hours to kill. We had the taxi driver drop us off at an all-night "Grudo Hospital" a couple of blocks from the train station. When I asked for a menu, they brought me a bowl of Menudo. Menudo is the cure-all for being grudo. As we were not hungover, and Sonia detests Menudo, I was able to ascertain that they had no menu. They only had what was on offer. Marie and James slept their exhausted little bodies through this lively exchange. We moved over to the ticketing window at the train station and managed to be first in line after placing

Marie and James to continue their slumber. When the ticketing agent opened his window and asked us how many tickets we required, we told him, two adults and two children. He said we were in the wrong line as he pointed to the window next to his. We moved over to the unmanned window as he rolled his chair over to serve us. This farce was a quaint reminder of cross-cultural patience.

An exciting train ride was exited at Bahuichivo, where we were able to catch a shuttle to Urique. The ride was rather crowded, and Marie was welcomed to sit on the lap of a willing Abuela as James sat on mine. Veronica was so welcoming at Entré Amigos, and we proceeded to make ourselves at home. We hiked down south to Guapalina, where cold sodas at the tienda went perfectly with the very warm and sunny day. We pushed irrigation drainage to the west and marveled at all the canyon bottom agriculture that was going on. The distance to Guadalupe Coronado necessitated hitching a ride in the back of a willing pickup truck. Cold sodas available there made for a great accompaniment to our packed lunches. James set a personal record of wiping out five times in his zest-for-life frenetic running about. Sonia drying his tears and administering first aid was so poignant.

Back in Creel, we were able to secure a ride to Magurarichi, where we headed straight for La Casa Lucero to rent a room. Perfect weather made for explorations of the surrounding countryside. Sadly, it also made Sonia receive a righteous sunburn. Running into Mexican troops brought home the point that the war on drugs was on. The lieutenant told me that growers were infesting the Rio Otero. The middle of the night saw Sonia doing battle with a large scorpion as she had gotten up to take a pee. My hiking boot served well as her weapon of choice, and the flattened alacran provided a visual to go along with her exclamation of "There!" The Hot Springs Resort being constructed up the road provided a really tranquil picnic destination where we could swim in their large hot spring Alberca.

Walking back into town, I admonished high-energy James to stick close to us. As he ran ahead, a dog darted out and bit him on the leg. I was able to flag down the town constable, who was able to take James and me on his four-wheeler to the village clinic, where the resident doctor cleaned the bite and administered a Gamma Globulin shot. He advised a return to the United States where James could receive the rabies series of shots. His getting chomped was optimal timing because it was already time to head home. What was nonoptimal was going to be dropping him off with his mother in Silver City, with instructions to get him the rabies shots.

Passing slowly through Chihuahua City the bus pulled up to a street stop where I saw a pretty young woman obviously jonesing for a fix. As her lithe and tired-looking body rhythmically jerked about, I wonder when her selling her body and soul would come to an end. My memories of her from 2002 quickly gave way to thoughts of just getting home.

Epilogue:
Las Barrancas Del Cobre

Canyons are physiographic features of the Earth's surface where erosion of the crust caused by the relentless flow of wind and water over spans of time immemorial lead to incredible features that can boggle the mind. Rampant thoughts have a parallel effect on the human psyche. We let mentation replay and replay until we end up in ruts. The ruts wear deeper and deeper with the passage of time, ultimately leading to a place so profound that it is practically impossible to climb out of. The choice becomes to just continue descending until a sea-level equivalent is reached while avoiding going under, or rock bottoms that lead to absolutely nowhere good.

The canyon years occurred at a time in my life when I ran to stand still. I didn't so much set out to be a canyon explorer, as I was just an intellectual outdoorsman in search of wonder. That child fishing on the Gulf of Mexico is where my eternal Earth-bound self belonged. The memories of that life present images of perhaps the happiest I have ever been in this life. Yes, I have known all other manners and times of joy. Having my children completed a part of me that had acted as a sieve that let too much out. That I gravitated toward Early Childhood Education proved to be serendipitous, as I have lived a life of seeking a metaphysical understanding of a holistic reality that transcends the purely scientific way of perceiving things. Cause and effect, subjective and objective, malevolent and benign, life and death, all represent parts of a puzzle unsolved. A puzzle with pieces strewn about the universe. A universe at once within and without.

The physical life transports consciousness through a world of possibilities beyond the mere stuff of stars. The coalescing of the dust to dust into an awakening of thought as life experiences the universe for a universe that slumbers without thought. Life is the vehicle of subjective reality. The realm of the physical, like hunger and pain. Like sorrow and joy. No matter where you go, there you are.

Dreams represent the greatest attribute of the human mind. In dreams, we create a subjective reality that has no need to be objectified. Dreams are a private decompression of experience and thought. Dreams are at once conscious and subconscious. When engaged in the art of living, we should dream big dreams and live life large. Thoughts of traversing all three sister barrancas were supplemented by the many dreams that companioned the reality of realizing such a feat. I began life as an infant in a crib that could not constrain me as I continually scaled the high rail to alight on the waiting ground. The awaiting Earth.

CPSIA information can be obtained
at www.ICGtesting.com
Printed in the USA
BVHW051919280623
666508BV00004B/148